Veggie Village and the Great & Dangerous Jungle

AN ALLEGORY

BEN R. PETERS

Veggie Village and the Great and Dangerous Jungle
© 2009 by Ben R. Peters

Author grants permission for any non-commercial reproduction to promote the Kingdom of God. All rights reserved.

Published by
KINGDOM SENDING CENTER
P. O. Box 25
Genoa, IL 60135

www.kingdomsendingcenter.org
ben.peters@kingdomsendingcenter.org

ISBN 13: 978-0-9789884-5-6
ISBN 10: 0-9789884-5-0

All scripture quotations, unless otherwise indicated, are taken from the New King James Version. © 1982 by Thomas Nelson, Inc. Used by permission. All rights reserved.

Cover image © 2009 Adam Kmiolek
Cover design and book interior by *www.ChristianBookDesign.com*

Contents

Preface	THE VISION	5
Chapter One	THE JUNGLE	7
Chapter Two	VEGGIE VILLAGE	13
Chapter Three	THE YOUNG RADICALS	19
Chapter Four	THE ALLY	25
Chapter Five	THE STRATEGY	31
Chapter Six	THE NAME	41
Chapter Seven	THE WELL	47
Chapter Eight	THE SURPRISE	59
Chapter Nine	THE ATTACK	69
Chapter Ten	THE FRUIT	79
Chapter Eleven	THE CONFRONTATION	87
Chapter Twelve	THE FRUIT OF THE FRUIT	103
	ADDENDUM	107

Preface

THE VISION

This book was birthed through a quick vision I received while in Hamilton, Ontario, Canada, in the late Spring of 2009. I saw a large jungle with some spaces cleared that were clearly vegetable gardens. I asked the Lord for understanding.

God spoke to my spirit that the vegetable garden represented the church and the jungle represented the world. He reminded me that parents often instruct their children, "Eat your vegetables, they're good for you." When church becomes more of a religion than a relationship, it becomes like eating vegetables. We're told to do good things like read your Bible, pray and go to church because it's good for us.

However, God wants to win the lost, and it's not that easy to get people to come and eat with us if we are having nothing but vegetables. He wants us to partake of His spiritual fruit and power and then serve it to others so that the very nature and loving character of God, our wonderful Father and Giver of Life, is revealed.

The jungle, with all of its dangers, certainly provides a lot more adventure than a village that grows nothing but vegetables. People would rather live dangerously than be bored. They would rather take their chances with the vast majority, including their friends and relatives, than live what seems to be the weird existence of a small minority.

God created the church to be the most exciting place on earth. He has given us both the fruit and the gifts of the Holy Spirit, as well as the pleasures of His very presence. "In His presence is fullness of joy, and at His right hand are pleasures forevermore." (Psalms 16:11)

As you read this story, you will see how spiritual fruit and gifts are totally intertwined. In the final chapter, this fascinating relationship will be explained. Until then, enjoy the story!

I also want to clarify that I do not justify a spirit of rebellion or disrespect for elders. The heroes in this story always attempted to be respectful, but they are clearly saying, "We must obey God rather than men."

As Christian leaders, we must discern the difference between a rebellious spirit and a passion for truth and righteousness.

Chapter One

The Jungle

Once upon a time, not very long ago, in a land not very far away, there was a great and dangerous jungle. The jungle was huge and stretched for thousands of miles in every direction. It was very deep and very dark and full of people from many different cultures who spoke many different languages. Some were highly educated and sophisticated, while others were very primitive, and lacked any formal education, living day-to-day from hand-to-mouth.

Some sections of the jungle had highly developed systems of communication and transportation with modern conveniences and technological developments of every kind, while other sections relied on footpaths and human messengers for their transportation and communication needs. In the same way, sophisticated business and commerce existed in some parts of the jungle. In other parts, bartering for simple items such as food and clothing was the common means of commerce.

The diet of the jungle dwellers was somewhat limited. Without much sunlight, many plants would not grow. Hunting was popular, as many wild animals inhabited the jungle and could be hunted for fresh meat. Monkey meat and wild boar were two of the jungle's greatest delicacies. Staples included roots and the bark of some trees, as well as some leaves and flowers that grew in the heart of the jungle.

Darkness

The one thing that all regions had in common was that the jungle was very dark. Very little sunshine could penetrate the thick green foliage to reach the jungle floor. The more developed parts of the jungle had artificial light to alleviate the eyestrain, but few jungle residents ever saw the glory of the light of the sun in its full splendor. If sunlight ever did find its way through the foliage, the people would run because they feared being blinded by it. At night, the moon and stars were almost never seen. With the exception of those small areas where artificial light was produced, intense darkness covered the jungle. In the poorer parts of the jungle, candles were lit sparingly, as wax was difficult to obtain.

Fear

As a result of the deep darkness, fear and danger lurked in every part of the jungle from east to west and from north to south. There were no police to protect the residents. This was a jungle and there was no central government to provide security. Those sections that were more prosperous tried to protect themselves, but bandits and wild men roamed freely throughout the jungle. The wildly growing foliage provided great cover for desperate criminals who could hide like animals and strike when it was least expected. No one was safe and many people had their possessions stolen. Others were killed and many had their homes and valuables destroyed by lawless men.

In addition to wild and evil men, there were many other creatures of the jungle to contend with. From swarms of biting insects to large predators like lions, leopards, tigers and boa constrictors, the jungle was fraught with danger and unexpected death in the form of a hungry beast or a disease-carrying mosquito.

From the most developed to the most primitive sections of this jungle, fear reigned over its inhabitants. The more a person possessed, the greater the fear of losing it all. The poorer jungle dwellers, with few possessions, feared sudden attacks by enemy tribes, which could cost them their lives or the lives of family members. Tribal warfare had gone on for many generations, and there was no reasonable end in sight.

Depression

Along with fear, the great and overpowering feeling of depression covered the jungle with a thick cloud of hopelessness and despair. Even the wealthier residents knew that the future had no guarantees for them or their children. They had seen many of their relatives killed or robbed of all their possessions. Sudden diseases had taken some out, while others had succumbed to wild animals that stealthily roamed the jungle killing and devouring the weak or unprotected until they, themselves, were killed and devoured.

Suicide

Depression and fear brought many to the conclusion that life was just not worth the effort required to survive. If they were going to lose their lives sooner or later anyhow, they might as well choose for themselves how they preferred to die. Although it added a huge burden of emotional pain to their families, many young people chose suicide as their means of escaping the jungle.

Jungle Juice

The residents had long since discovered the special effects that some plants had when treated and prepared in certain ways. To overcome their depression and fear, most residents drank a substance that had significant mind-altering impact, which they specially prepared and guarded from would-be thieves. Drinking this jungle juice gave them a temporary feeling of euphoria, but it also created other problems, which added to the long list of things that they already had to deal with.

These problems resulted from a blurred mind and a lack of rational restraint in their behavior among friends, family and enemies. Many fights broke out, causing physical and emotional injury and the destruction of property. Children were filled with more fear than ever when they saw their parents, aunts and uncles and others in their homes imbibing the homemade, but very intoxicating beverage.

Along with the jungle juice, they discovered that certain plants or weeds could be smoked for an additional high. Unfortunately, smoking these plants not only altered their minds, but they were extremely habit-forming. Many spent their time finding these rare species of plants and selling them to those who felt they could not live without them. The end result for those who used these substances was more depression and hopelessness than they had before using them.

ADVENTURE

On the positive side, the jungle was a place filled with adventure, especially for the young. As always, adventure and danger go hand in hand. There were many creatures to hunt, while at the same time, some of those creatures could be hunting the hunters. With the many trees and huge vines to climb and hide in, anyone looking for adventure could surely find it. It was a great place to play tricks on friends and annoy or attack enemies.

The boys invented games of skill and luck, trying to be the toughest and bravest. The girls played house and pretended to be grown up mamas. The girls often played hide-and-seek with the boys, and there was no better place to play that game than their own jungle. Sadly, many of their games ended with someone getting hurt or even killed, but that was life in the jungle and everyone was used to it.

The Jungle had a Name

The jungle had a very interesting name, which was accepted in every dark corner of its length and breadth. The name of the jungle was Normal. Most Normal Jungle dwellers knew no other way of life, and the life that they lived there was considered by all to be very normal.

Many generations had lived and died in Normal Jungle. The elders who had survived a few decades of jungle life had many stories to tell of their experiences and exploits. In addition, they passed on the stories they had been told by the elders of generations past. Of course, the older the stories were, the more embellished they became, and the younger children would sit in awe as their elders shared the most amazing tales of adventure that had occurred in various parts of Normal Jungle.

Every now and then, one of the elders would mention a part of the jungle that few of them had ever visited. In fact, it was not really a part of the jungle, although it was situated within its larger borders. It was a small patch of land, compared to the vastness of Normal Jungle, but it was nothing like the rest of the jungle, and it sounded like a very scary place to those who had never visited it. Those who had seen this unusual and not normal place would always warn others to stay away from it.

The elders spoke of the open sky above this patch of land and the bright ball of fire that would burn anyone who left the safety of the jungle foliage. The natives of this place were also very strange, and every so often they would try to convince the Normal people to stay and live with them in this hot and barren land. When the elders talked about this place, those who listened were filled with fear, and only the bravest young Normal residents had any desire to visit this very strange place.

Chapter Two

VEGGIE VILLAGE

The place they were talking about was known as Veggie Village, which was a unique settlement of strong, brave and rather proud people, who had a history of being different from the people of Normal Jungle. Veggie Village was inhabited by the descendants of an ancient people who had experienced and witnessed some very amazing things in generations past.

The ancient scrolls that the Veggie Village elders read to their families on a regular basis were filled with stories of the most exciting adventures that men on earth had ever experienced. These almost unbelievable stories were even stranger and more difficult to imagine than the stories that were told by Normal Jungle elders to their children.

PAST MIRACLES

According to the ancient scrolls, their ancestors had experienced events that were almost magical. According to these stories, people who had been killed by evil men or by sickness and disease had come back to life. Others, who had been crippled from birth, had suddenly begun to walk. Blind eyes had opened and deaf ears were instantly made to hear clearly. Great men and women had used a special power to accomplish such magical feats. Their names were clearly recorded in the ancient scrolls that the village elders read.

Although it was somewhat difficult for the younger folk to understand, it seemed that the Central Character in these ancient scrolls had taught the people how to grow special fruit trees. If the fruit of these trees was eaten, then it would give them special power to do the impossible things that were written about in the scrolls. Unfortunately, however, these particular trees, they were told, had long since died out and had become extinct.

According to the village elders, the villagers had been instructed by the Founder to commemorate these miracles in holy ceremonies at least once a week and to live their lives in certain ways that would please Him. It was said in the sacred scrolls that He would be watching them from a place that they could not see with their natural eyes. It was also said that some day He would return again to reward those who had served Him well and had been faithful to obey His instructions.

Indeed, according to those same scrolls, the great Founder of their village had Himself experienced the miracle of resurrection and had left instructions for His disciples, who would carry on the memories of His life and teachings. And so, the story was told, that if they pleased Him well, they too could experience a resurrection from death in a different land that was much more enjoyable than Veggie Village.

VEGGIE VILLAGE QUISINE

As indicated by the name, Veggie Village, the fruit trees had been replaced by a variety of garden vegetables that grew in the ground and provided no shade or protection from the glaring sun. All of the residents of Veggie Village were required to spend a fair amount of their time caring for and harvesting their vegetable garden.

The diet of Veggie Village was, as you could have guessed, the veggies that they grew. These vegetables were not the tastiest morsels on the planet, but all Veggie Village residents had been told as young children that veggies were good for their physical and spiritual health, and they would protect them from disease and the evil curses of the jungle people. The children were always told, "Eat your vegetables. They will make you strong and wise like the village elders."

Tradition and Simplicity

Veggie Village folk liked to keep life simple. While some of the regions of Normal Jungle had advanced technology and communications networks, Veggie Village tended to live in the past and resisted the temptation to modernize. The whole focus of Veggie Village was keeping traditions of the past in order to please the Original Founder.

The inhabitants of Veggie Village were truly far better off in most ways than those in Normal Jungle. They lived with much less fear and depression, most of them lived much longer than Normal Jungle dwellers, and they had hope for a happier future when they died.

Reaching out to Normal Jungle

Some Veggie Village dwellers were very concerned about those who lived nearby in Normal Jungle. They had heard from the ancient scrolls that they should warn those living there that they would experience terrible consequences in the future if they didn't leave their jungle and move to Veggie Village.

Throughout the history of Veggie Village, there had always been a few brave and devoted followers of the Original Founder who had risked their lives venturing into Normal Jungle. They tried to persuade the inhabitants to leave their jungle lives and to come and live with them in Veggie Village.

Some of these brave souls had been attacked and a number had died. But some of these excursions were more fruitful. Occasionally, they would find one or two desperate folk who were in such bad shape that they had nothing to lose. These rescue missions, when successful, brought great excitement to Veggie Village. There would be some happy celebrations, and the very finest vegetables would be served to all.

However, there were very few village residents who considered it their responsibility to rescue folk from Normal Jungle. They felt that everyone had a free will, and they chose to live where they did. The consequences of their behavior were not really anyone's problem but their own.

In fact, since a few jungle dwellers had made raids and attacked members of Veggie Village during the dark nights, some Veggie Village dwellers had advocated building walls around their community. In some sections, the local elders had agreed with this idea, and walls had been erected in these sections.

The overall picture of Veggie Village was that it was a place of relative peace and safety. The dangers were far less than in Normal Jungle and the life expectancy was certainly a lot higher.

On the other hand, life was also more on the dull side. Except for the few who made the effort to rescue Normal Jungle dwellers, there was little excitement or adventure in Veggie Village. Everyone went about their routine and kept the traditions of their fathers. There was little creative energy left after working under the hot sun day after day, and meals were always pretty boring. However, as they often reminded themselves and each other, they could be stuck in Normal Jungle, where life could really be atrocious and filled with extreme danger.

Problems in Veggie Village

Not everything was totally perfect in Veggie Village either. Time had passed since the ancient scrolls had been written, and different elders had risen up over the centuries with special revelation, according to them, to interpret the ancient scrolls. These revelations usually had to do with which veggies were important to eat if one wanted a very long life.

Not everyone would accept these new revelations, and divisions in

Veggie Village began to occur as a result. There were soon large sections of Veggie Village named after various village elders or the particular vegetable that they felt was the most nutritious and essential to a happy life. Their faithful followers continued to believe what they had been taught long after the elders had died.

In fact, they not only held fast to the doctrine of their favorite ancient elder, but they often had debates and squabbles about which ancient elder was right and which was a heretic. These disagreements had gotten so strong in the past that some had even died to defend their positions.

Most of the time, the residents of the various sections of Veggie Village could get along and coexist, but they seldom worked together in great harmony, as the Original Founder of their village had intended. Instead, there seemed to be a strong competitive drive amongst their leaders to grow their own spheres of influence and gain greater control over Veggie Village.

This condition had existed in Veggie Village for some time, and, like the jungle dwellers, the Veggie Village dwellers also considered it normal. Most of them expected life to continue as it had for generations. Few had ever even considered the possibility of life as it once had been when the great Founder of their village had lived.

But, there were a few...

Chapter Three

THE YOUNG RADICALS

And those few were a great and continuous irritation to the various village elders. They were mostly quite young, restless and considered very radical. They continually challenged their elders with questions like, "How do we know our village has to be like this? What if we discovered some seeds from the ancient trees that used to grow here?"

QUESTIONS WITHOUT ANSWERS

Their questions never received satisfactory answers. They were usually told that their questions were ridiculous. Why didn't they just accept what had happened as the will of the Original Founder who, after all, was watching over them and had the power to do whatever He wanted.

Many of these young radicals had tried to impact some of the jungle regions by taking their veggies for the natives to taste. They had found their efforts almost totally rejected and a waste of time. They wondered what it would be like if they had some of the ancient fruit to take with them into the jungle. But the elders kept telling them that the fruit was gone forever and they needed to accept reality.

But the young radicals, while trying to show due respect to their elders, could not accept their dream-destroying words. Some of the young radicals began sneaking into the buildings where the ancient scrolls were kept, and they made copies of the scrolls so that they could read them for themselves. This was not acceptable to the village elders and many were punished for these acts of rebellion. However, nothing could stop these seekers of the truth, and their numbers and determination continued to grow.

The village elders disapproved of their reading the ancient scrolls, and they had repeatedly told them, "You don't have the wisdom or experience to understand those scrolls. Leave the interpretation of the scrolls to us. We are the only ones who can interpret them."

However, the young radicals were never satisfied with that answer. If the elders were so qualified to interpret the ancient scrolls, why did so many of them have different interpretations of the same scrolls? Maybe it was time for a newer and fresher approach by some bold young minds that were not bound by long-held traditions of men.

Hungry for Truth

Radicals from the various sections of Veggie Village began to meet together and share their excitement about restoring Veggie Village to its original state. The truth was that the name of their village had not always been Veggie Village. That name had become accepted long ago, since growing veggies had become the main occupation of their village.

In fact, the original name of their village was very difficult to discover. The ancient scrolls had not clearly stated it, and the young radicals considered it a treasure worth hunting for. If they could discover the original name of their village, they might have the clue they needed to restore the village to its original glory.

Their primary goal was to search out where they could find seeds from the original fruit trees that had grown there. Many of them were convinced deep down inside that they still existed and were not really extinct. Somewhere in the ancient scrolls there had to be more clues to the secret hiding place of this ancient treasure.

No matter how much persecution and mocking they received, these radical truth-seekers and treasure hunters would not be stopped. Many times they would stay up late into the night searching the scrolls, and then they would have to get up early in the morning to work the fields in the hot sun. It was difficult, but they kept feeling that their breakthrough had to be near. One of these days, the clue would be found that would lead them directly to the wonderful treasure.

Past Transformation

The ancient scrolls documented a great revolutionary transformation of the territory they now lived in during the days of their Original Founder and his followers. The vegetable gardens had been overshadowed by the wonderful fruit trees that thrived throughout their village, and the fruit brought great excitement to those living in their community and in Normal Jungle as well.

The jungle dwellers had responded to the beautiful, sweet fruit offered by the villagers, and many left their old way of life to become disciples or followers of the Original Founder of the village. During those exciting days, many terrible diseases were cured, and everyone in the jungle heard amazing stories about the power of the special fruit. Although some did not believe the stories, everyone was aware that something unusual was happening in their world.

It was also clear that much of the jungle had once been radically changed by the fruit-growing disciples. The jungle had given up much of its territory to grow more of this beautiful, life-changing fruit. Jungle foliage had been cleared to make room for the fruit trees. As a result, more and more light had invaded the jungle, transforming it in many ways. Crime and violence had diminished since the darkness had receded, and more and more people had relocated to the new regions of light.

The young radicals began to wonder what had happened, and how things had changed so radically since ancient times. The answer was not immediately apparent, but gradually they began to piece the many little clues together. After awhile, they came to some very important conclusions.

Decline of the Original Village

The memories of the Original Founder had begun to fade with succeeding generations. The scrolls could not be read by many residents because they were not literate, and they depended upon their leaders to read and interpret the scrolls for them. The problem was that the intimate knowledge of the heart and character of the Original Founder had diminished, and their leaders had less passion and love for Him than the first disciples.

As a result, they began to interpret the words of the scrolls through their own experiences. Certain passages were skipped over because they didn't seem relevant to their world. Since the people trusted the elders to keep them informed, they blindly followed the changes that were occurring little by little.

In addition, as more and more inhabitants of Normal Jungle had accepted their teachings, there had been less opposition and persecution. Without the persecution, increased passivity and complacency occurred, and then it seemed that the presence and power of the Original Founder wasn't as significant. The village elders then began to increasingly accept the comforts of life as normal. They enjoyed their positions of authority and honor, and they spent less time seeking the adventurous life that the Original Founder's disciples had pursued.

As the love grew colder for the Original Founder, Veggie Village residents began to neglect the fruit trees that He had planted for them. They still enjoyed the fruit, but they no longer saved the seeds or planted them in the ground. Although the fruit was still tasty, it did not seem to produce the same results in those who consumed it. Many of their attempts to do miraculous things produced so few results that they eventually quit trying, resigned to the fact that this was not part of their calling.

Because the fruit was not tended, it was getting smaller and less abundant on the trees. Before long, the fruit had almost stopped growing completely. As a substitute for the lack of fruit, many village leaders began to emphasize the importance of growing and eating vegetables. The barren fruit trees were taking up too much space, so they were cut down and used for firewood. The roots of the trees were pulled out of the ground, which was cultivated so it would be fit for growing good vegetables.

Hope for Restoration

This was all that the young village radicals were able to discover after researching the history of Veggie Village from the village archives. They believed that the seeds from the fruit of those special trees had been saved by someone, and if they searched diligently enough, then those seeds could be found and planted in the ground. Although they couldn't explain why, they were certain that if they could plant the ancient seeds, then they could once again produce the amazing results experienced by the disciples of the Original Founder.

What they didn't know was that a young disciple, named Fearless Dreamer, had saved seeds from all of the fruit trees long before the village elders had decided to chop the trees down. As his name indicates, he was a dreamer who had received a very special dream. The Original Founder had appeared to him in a dream and had spoken to him in a very sober tone of voice.

"Fearless Dreamer," He said, "you have been chosen to preserve the special fruit that you have tasted. You have experienced the release of power yourself to do supernatural things that honor Me. I want you to save several seeds of each tree and store them in an earthen vessel with a tight seal, so that no air or water can penetrate it for many centuries. When you have gathered seeds from all the fruit trees, I will tell you where to hide them. For the day will come when the trees will be cut down, and there will be no longer any fruit in this village."

This dream shook Fearless Dreamer to the very core of his soul, and he obediently did exactly as he was told.

The next night, when the villagers had all retired, Fearless Dreamer began the sacred assignment that had been entrusted to him. With just the light of the half-moon and the Evening Star, he found the fruit trees that were still growing in various parts of the village. Under each tree he found the precious fruit, which had fallen to the ground because no one had picked it. He placed each piece of fruit carefully in his basket and hurried home where he could extract and preserve the seeds.

One by one the fruit was cut open and the seeds were removed. Fearless Dreamer set them out to dry near his little fireplace. During the next few days, he allowed no one in his house, lest they should ask questions and mock him. Finally, when the seeds were ready for preservation, he found the perfect earthen vessel and put the many seeds into it.

With a special sealant known to only a few craftsmen, Fearless Dreamer sealed the lid. With a silent prayer, he requested protection for these precious seeds until the appointed time chosen by the Original Founder. Fully aware of the importance of this project, Fearless Dreamer went to bed wondering when he would receive his next instructions.

That very night in a dream, the Original Founder gave Fearless Dreamer clear instructions as to where the seeds should be buried. The Original Founder also told him that someday a group of young radicals would be searching for those seeds. When they found them, they would grow the ancient fruit again, and this fruit would produce even greater results than it had at the beginning. Faithful Dreamer once again carefully followed the instructions he was given, and he hid the precious seeds in a secret hiding place during the night under the light of the moon.

For centuries the seeds had remained hidden in the secret hiding place, waiting to be discovered at the right time by the right group of passionate young radicals who were willing to search until they found the treasure.

Chapter Four

THE ALLY

The more often the young radicals got together, the more determined they were to find the ancient seeds and once again grow the wonderful fruit with the amazing powers. They knew there was a mystery to be solved, but the village elders, with the exception of Patient Hope, were not interested in solving it.

There was something uniquely different about Patient Hope. He was one of the oldest of the village elders, a quiet man with few words, but when he spoke, people listened. In his youth, Patient Hope had been considered radical too, because he also believed in the restoration of the ancient fruit, and he had stirred up quite a fuss with the village elders of his day. However, as time went on, Patient Hope became resigned to the fact that he might have to wait for the fulfillment of his dream. He consequently became more focused on knowing and understanding the Original Founder of the village, and the more he learned, the more his personal love and appreciation for Him grew.

For most Veggie Village residents, the Original Founder was someone they had learned about, but very few had experienced a real deep love for Him or had actually encountered Him in a personal way. Most of them tried hard to follow the rules taught by the village elders, but they never really felt they were doing enough to please the Original Founder, who was presumably always watching them.

However, Patient Hope was one of the few exceptions. When he could get away from everyone else, he loved to softly sing the songs that he had learned in his childhood. When he couldn't remember any more songs, he made up his own using simple words, accompanied by a simple melody. The theme of all his songs was his great love for the Original Founder, how much He meant to him, and how he desired to please Him.

SPECIAL VISITATIONS

It was during one of these sweet times that Patient Hope heard that still small voice in his heart. It was so real that it was almost audible. The voice said, "Patient Hope, you were well named. If you are patient and don't lose hope, you will live to see your dream come true."

The experience shook Patient Hope to the very core of his soul, just like Faithful Dreamer's dramatic dream experience had shaken him. Had the Original Founder actually spoken to him? There seemed to be no doubt about it. From that moment on, Patient Hope said very little about the ancient fruit to the others, but he never lost confidence that his dream would be fulfilled in his lifetime.

As Patient Hope journeyed through life, he observed a few other young people who asked some of the same radical questions that he had asked his elders years before. Each time a younger radical would arise in the village, he wondered, "Is this the one that will change everything about Veggie Village?" However, one by one, each of the young radicals had gradually accepted the "normal" way of life in Veggie Village.

Now there was something special about the latest group of young radicals. In his spirit, Patient Hope felt a resurgence of his youthful passion for the marvelous fruit with its amazing power. For some time, while all the other village elders grumbled about the young radicals and their "rebellious" attitudes, Patient Hope just observed them with great interest. He didn't want to give them false hope, nor did he want to create more strife with the other village elders by supporting the young rebels.

Patient Hope wasn't getting any younger, and he spent as much time as possible in solitude talking to the Original Founder and listening to see if He would talk to him one more time. He kept asking, "Is this the time? Are these the ones who will bring the restoration of the fabulous fruit?"

One day when he was packing up to go to home, he finally heard that still, small voice again. "Patient Hope, the time has come. Join your heart to the young radicals and encourage them to pursue their dreams, no matter what. They will be successful if they don't give up."

Patient Hope stood there stunned and speechless. Then pent-up emotions began to find expression like he had never experienced before. The quiet, white-haired elder began to sob uncontrollably for several minutes, and then he began to softly sing songs of worship and praise to the Original Founder. He thanked Him for speaking clearly to him and for the exciting confirmation that this was now the time and this very group of radicals would actually find the seeds and restore the fruit. His life-long dream would finally be fulfilled. How could he thank Him enough?

Patient Hope had been observing the young radicals long enough to know who the leaders were. The young man, who seemed to be the most determined to find the seeds, was called Extreme Courage. He was respectful to the elders, but he did not accept their advice to give up his search for the seeds. He was a young man on a mission, who could not be distracted by anything that came his way.

The next day, after he had heard that still, small voice, Patient Hope noticed Extreme Courage coming out of his house with two friends and fellow-radicals named Strong Support and Gentle Compassion. Patient Hope walked over and asked to speak with them. The young radicals looked at each other wondering what to expect from yet another village elder who wanted to speak to them. What kind of a lecture would they be getting this time?

Reluctantly and respectfully, the three young people agreed to hear what Patient Hope had to say to them. Patient Hope was invited into the house, and they sat down around a simple kitchen table and asked what was on his mind. They were totally surprised by what he had to say.

"You don't know this, my young friends, but several decades ago, I was a young radical on the same quest that you are on. I was put down by my village elders and persecuted for my belief that the ancient fruit could be restored to our village. I tried to stay true to my dream, but I had grown weary without much support until I heard a voice in my heart telling me that I would live to see the day that my dream would be fulfilled. I have hung on to that dream for a long time."

"I have been waiting for confirmation from the Original Founder that the time had come and the right group of radical dreamers had arrived on the scene. Yesterday, after all these years, I heard that voice again, and I received clear confirmation that now is the time, and that you are the ones to find the hidden treasure after all these centuries."

"So please know that I am ready to work with you, and I offer you whatever I have, including my knowledge of the ancient manuscripts and the stories that my own grandfather passed on to me. I have never been more excited, and I am confident that we are on the threshold of breakthrough for the restoration of the wonderful fruit trees that were planted by the Original Founder. I believe that if we work together, and if we don't quit when things get difficult, we will be successful."

When Patient Hope finished speaking, the three young treasure seekers looked at each other once again, this time with their eyes bulging and their mouths open. This could be the break they were crying out for. Finally, a true village elder believed in them and was willing to work with them.

Extreme Courage quickly regained his composure. "Patient Hope, you have no idea how much this means to us. We are just overwhelmed! I know we will be successful, and it will go much faster with your help. I know you have read and studied the ancient scrolls long before we were born. Your knowledge will be a real asset to us. It is awesome that the Original Founder would speak to you about us and our quest for truth!"

"Yes, my dear friends," responded Patient Hope, "the Original Founder cares about us more than we know. I have grown closer to Him as the years have passed, and I know He wants you to discover the seeds more than you do. He wants us to pursue the truth at all costs. We must not quit or get discouraged. We have only just begun, but we will succeed!"

Time for Strategy

"When can we meet again for a strategy session?" piped up Strong Support, who had been silent until now. "I can't wait to get started."

Patient Hope replied, "Let's meet tomorrow night about two hours after sunset. Most of the village will be sleeping and we should be able to meet without anyone noticing us. Let's meet in the big old tool shed near the broccoli field at the edge of Normal Jungle. Get the word out to the other young radicals that you know you can trust."

"Sounds like a good plan!" said Extreme Courage.

"We'll all be there!" added Strong Support excitedly.

Gentle Compassion stepped close to Patient Hope and touched him on the shoulder. Her voice was soft and touched with deep emotion. "How can we thank you enough? None of the elders have ever given us any encouragement before. They have always fought against us. You have brought such great joy to our hearts today. I don't know what else to say."

With that said, the tears began to flow from her beautiful dark brown eyes. Patient Hope's eyes also became teary as he gently put his arm around her and spoke kindly to her, "I know how you feel, but I feel the same way. I owe so much to you, but we all owe everything to the Original Founder, who sacrificed everything to give us our village in the first place. Without Him we would have nothing."

Gentle Compassion nodded with the tears still flowing down her face. The two young men chimed in, "That's right, Patient Hope! We owe everything to Him."

Chapter Five

THE STRATEGY

The old tool shed was packed with young radicals and excitement charged the atmosphere. Patient Hope cautioned them to keep their voices down, and then he began to speak softly but with a clear, discernable excitement in his voice.

"I know you are all very excited, but no one is more excited than I am because I have been waiting for this day for several decades. The Original Founder of Veggie Village has let me know that this is the time that I have been waiting for, and you are the young radicals that will restore this village to its original greatness."

"We have gathered here tonight because I believe that as we unite our zeal and knowledge with understanding that we will be blessed with the strategy that we need for a complete restoration of our village. I see that your leader, Extreme Courage, has brought a copy of some of the sacred scrolls with him. I think it would be appropriate that we read a small portion before we continue with our discussion. So, if you don't mind, Extreme Courage, would you please read a portion at this time."

Extreme Courage said, "It will be my honor to read from the scroll." He quickly found a passage that he had been studying recently. He began to read slowly and emphatically. The passage he read talked about Living Water and how it quenched the thirst of everyone who drank it. Just one drink of this water reproduced a Living Well within the person who drank it. Then the person who drank it would be a source of Living Water for others."

Extreme Courage stopped reading and addressed the village elder, "Patient Hope, do you have any insights into the meaning of this passage? It has intrigued me for some time now, and I feel like it is a special clue for us, but I just can't solve it."

"I think you are on to something, Extreme Courage," said Patient Hope. "The Original Founder loved to talk about Living Water and He promised to provide Living Water to all of His followers once He was gone."

"In fact, there are some other secret village scrolls, which only a few have ever seen. It was implied within these scrolls that the Original Founder had poured this Living Water on those original fruit trees. These were ordinary trees that had never produced much fruit in the past, but they produced amazing fruit when the Living Water was poured on them. These trees reproduced themselves very quickly, and their village was full of fruit trees loaded with delicious fruit before long."

"This fruit was even taken to many citizens of Normal Jungle. The followers of the Original Founder established new villages everywhere they went, and they planted fruit trees throughout the new villages. The jungle was cleared and the light shone brightly on the new villages. But for some reason, over a period of time, most of the new villages lost interest in the fruit and were either swallowed up by Normal Jungle or they developed into villages like ours. Some think these villages still exist in various regions, but no one from our village knows for sure."

Strong Support couldn't hold back his excitement. "I think we need to find the source of that Living Water. Surely the Original Founder wouldn't give us the seeds from the fruit trees without giving us the Living Water to produce the special fruit."

"You could be right, my friend," declared Extreme Courage. "We need to expand our search to include the fruit seeds and the Living Water."

Gentle Compassion responded, "I agree, Extreme Courage. We need the Living Water. I sense in my own spirit that the Living Water may be even more important than the fruit itself. Without it there would be no fruit of any value."

Extreme Courage nodded and smiled at her. "You have a lot of wisdom and discernment. Thanks for sharing that. I do believe you are right on in your evaluation of the situation."

"There is one more thing we need to search for," added Patient Hope. "And that is the original name of our village. I believe that if we could discover that name, it would be another clue for the restoration of our village. I don't know why that name is still a mystery, but I will diligently search all the ancient scrolls I can get my hands on for clues."

"And we will search for more clues regarding the Living Water and the hidden seeds," added Extreme Courage. "Gentle Compassion, you can take some friends and focus on the Living Water, and Strong Support, you can do the same regarding the hidden seeds. I will keep in touch with both of you and we can keep up with each other's progress."

"That's a great idea," added Patient Hope, "you are showing great leadership ability. I know we are getting closer than ever to our dream, and when we finally achieve this great breakthrough, the world will never be the same. Let's bow our heads and give thanks to the Original Founder for leading us and giving us His wisdom."

Soon all the young radicals and Patient Hope were slipping out of the old tool shed into the darkness of the night, with only a waning crescent moon in the western sky to give them light. They hadn't solved the mystery, but they all felt like they were a giant step closer, thanks to the wisdom and experience of their unexpected ally, Patient Hope.

ON THE HUNT FOR MORE CLUES

The next few days went by quickly. Everyone had a full schedule working in the vegetable gardens by day, in addition to reading scrolls and talking with others in the evenings. Patient Hope was on a hunt for the oldest village scrolls. These scrolls were held by many different village elders, most of whom were leaders of their section of Veggie Village.

Patient Hope had to be very creative in his reasons for asking to borrow them. As one of the oldest elders, he was well known by everyone in the village, but as far as he knew, none of the others were sympathetic to the cause of restoration. As a result, he had to word his requests very carefully. He had too much integrity to lie, but he had to keep his purpose a secret for the time being.

Asking the Original Founder for wisdom, Patient Hope decided to simply tell the other elders that he was doing some research for some memoirs he wanted to write before he died, and this was a true statement. Patient Hope planned on leaving behind the legacy of his journey for the next generation. He would share his entire story of being a young radical and about how he had finally connected with another group of young radicals in his later years. He also believed that the restoration of the ancient fruit trees would be in those memoirs.

Some of the elders were hesitant to let the scrolls out of their sight, but Patient Hope promised that he would return them the following day. Knowing that Patient Hope had always kept his word, each elder reluctantly placed the ancient scrolls gently in his hands. Mostly by the light of a couple of candles, Patient Hope read the ancient scrolls hour by hour until his vision was so blurred that he had to take a break to rest his eyes.

There were a few minor tidbits of information that Patient Hope had never read before, but there was nothing that told him the original name of Veggie Village, nor any leads about the Living Water or the fruit seeds. After a full week of research, Patient Hope was wondering if he was on the wrong track. Did he need to take a different approach? Would the Original Founder reveal the name through some other means?

There were still a few more scrolls that Patient Hope knew existed. He also knew that some of the elders who held these scrolls were the most antagonistic towards the young radicals. If they knew that he was aligned with them, they would never allow him to lay eyes on the scrolls. But, he also knew that he had to try until he had exhausted all resources available to him.

One day, Patient Hope walked from his northern section of Veggie Village that was the farthest south. The folk who lived in this section had some of the most extreme doctrines, and their chief elder had a reputation for being rather gruff and cold-hearted. The two elders had met only once or twice before, but they had very little in common. Patient Hope whispered a prayer to the Original Founder and knocked on the door.

PLEASANT SURPRISE

The elder's name was Rule Keeper. He was a tall, thin man with a long goatee. He greeted Patient Hope with a look of surprise, and then with unexpected friendliness he said, "Come in, come in! Please take that comfortable chair and I'll get you something to quench your thirst."

Returning with a tall glass of water, the elder spoke up, "Before you tell me why you have come this distance to see me, I have something to tell you."

Patient Hope was still in a state of shock and nodded politely.

"Last night I had the strangest dream. I dreamed that I was looking out across Veggie Village towards the north end where you come from. Suddenly, I saw trees springing up quickly all over Veggie Village, starting from the north and moving quickly towards our section in the south. As they sprang up close to me, I could see they were fruit trees, just loaded with luscious-looking fruit."

"Then I saw you picking the fruit, eating it and giving some to me. It was delicious and I immediately felt invigorated and on fire with zeal for our Original Founder. Then a voice told me to give you whatever you asked for, and I would be blessed because of the project you were involved in. Then the dream was over and I woke up shaking. As you probably know, I have a reputation for being rather stern and stubborn, but I feel like I am already a different man, even though it was just a dream. Can you tell me now what you have come for?"

Patient Hope responded, "This is so amazing that I am in shock! I should have trusted the Original Founder, since I did ask for His help. I guess my faith was not that strong."

"I have come to request an opportunity to read any of the ancient village scrolls that you may have in your possession. I am doing research for the memoirs that I am preparing to write. But since you have heard from the Original Founder yourself, I can tell you more if you promise to keep it a secret until we make it public."

"You can count on me to keep your secret", responded Rule Keeper. "What is your project all about?"

Patient Hope spent the next two hours sharing his personal testimony with the transformed elder. When he finished, the elder was weeping uncontrollably. When he finally gained his composure, he tried to explain his emotional reaction.

"I have been one of the strongest opponents of the young radicals. No one in our region has been allowed to even talk about the ancient fruit. I have been very harsh, and anyone who violated my rule was punished. Some submitted to me, while others fled to different regions of Veggie Village. Sadly, some even left the village completely and have gone to live in Normal Jungle."

"As I now realize what I have done, it is overwhelming how much harm I have done to the cause of the Original Founder, while trying to defend the doctrines of Veggie Village. I beg of you, Patient Hope, please forgive me and pray for me that I would be forgiven by the Original Founder, whom I have offended the most."

Patient Hope responded gently, "The Original Founder has already demonstrated His forgiveness, and He is giving you an opportunity to change your ways, as well as your heart. But I will pray for your heart to be healed from guilt and condemnation. The Original Founder taught his disciples to forgive as He forgives. His whole life and death focused on forgiveness rather than judgment."

"If you would like to join me in this great adventure, I would so appreciate your help in searching through your private collection of scrolls. We are looking for the original name of Veggie Village, as well as anything that comes up concerning the fruit trees and the Living Water that some scrolls have mentioned."

"That would be my great honor, Patient Hope," Rule Keeper replied. "I will bring them out of their hiding place. Please give me a few minutes and I will return with them."

Patient Hope sat in silence, but his mind was racing. Was this the breakthrough that he had been waiting for? How could it not be? The dream that this elder had received was not an everyday occurrence in Veggie Village. His prayers were being answered, and the Original Founder had given him an unexpected friend and helper in his quest for the return of the incredible glory of their original village.

When Rule Keeper finally returned, his countenance was aglow. In his arms was the largest collection of scrolls that Patient Hope had ever seen. "No one has read these for centuries," the slender elder declared. "The founder of our district of Veggie Village made it clear in his teachings and writings that we would only be confused if we read too much about the origins of our village. "

"He worked very hard to round up all the extra scrolls that were written in the early years of our village. He kept them under lock and key, and he passed them on to those who succeeded him. They have been under my protection for over thirty years. I know now that we have been in gross error, and I am willing to lay down my life to recover and restore what we have helped to conceal from the village."

Exploring the Scrolls

Patient Hope's hands trembled as he touched the precious scrolls. "Let's get started!" he said quietly. "I can't wait to see what has been hidden all these years."

Both elderly gentlemen began to silently pour over the scrolls, handling the parchments with extreme care. It wasn't long before valuable information began to leap out of the ancient text. Patient Hope could hardly contain his excitement, "I can't believe what I just read! I can't believe what I just read!"

FRUSTRATION AT HOME

Meanwhile, Strong Support and Gentle Compassion were working hard to find out more about the Living Water and the hidden seeds. Like Patient Hope, they had the feeling that they weren't getting anywhere. No matter how many of the Sacred Scrolls they read, they could find nothing about hidden seeds or the source of Living Water, other than the Original Founder, Himself.

A full week passed and there was still no breakthrough. Extreme Courage tried to keep them all encouraged. He reminded them that it would require patience and diligence to find the priceless treasure. He suggested that each of them pour out their hearts to the Original Founder, who was always listening to them.

Then one normal Veggie Village day, a young gal from the group approached Extreme Courage with a special glow of excitement on her countenance. She was one of the youngest radicals, named Quiet Meekness, and she motioned to him to step aside where she could tell him something in private.

"What's happening?" asked Extreme Courage.

A MOST SIGNIFICANT DREAM

"You'll never believe the dream that I had last night. I was walking through Veggie Village and suddenly I stumbled on something in the middle of the street, right in the heart of Veggie Village. You came up behind me and helped me back to my feet. Then you looked to see why I had stumbled. You saw something like a big circular lid covered with dirt. You began to work on it until you could lift it a little. You got excited and said that it was an ancient well. That was the end of the dream. I woke up really excited. I knew it was important and not just a crazy dream."

"That's amazing, Quiet Meekness. We must ask for more understanding, but I'm sure this could be the breakthrough we're looking for. We are looking for the source of Living Water, and then you have a dream about discovering a well in the heart of Veggie Village."

"Extreme Courage, I believe it's a real well that has been covered up for centuries. I know exactly where it is. I recognized the buildings all around it. I can take you there anytime you want to go."

"Okay, let's do it!" responded Extreme Courage with enthusiasm. "We will have to have a strategy though because we can't just dig up the center of the street in the middle of the day. We'll have to work in the middle of the night when everyone is asleep, and we'll have to have a plan in place in case someone does wake up from the noise. Then we'll have to gather some tools, ropes and candles, etc…"

"We'll have to plan things like clockwork, so we can come and go as quickly as possible. We'll have to try to cover our tracks, so that the street looks like nothing has taken place. I'll see if I can connect with Patient Hope, and let's gather at the tool shed again tomorrow night. I don't feel right about proceeding with anything until we've consulted with him. He's been very busy for the past week or so, and I pray that he is also having some success."

Chapter Six

The Name

"I just can't believe what I just read!" Patient Hope repeated the statement over and over. He was in a state of euphoria, as he enthusiastically read scroll after scroll. He had no idea there had been this much written about the village, in which he had lived his entire life, so many centuries before. More and more details were being revealed about life in the early days, and he was getting a better and clearer mental picture of his village as the Original Founder had designed it.

"This scroll talks about the amazing and miraculous works accomplished by those who ate the fruit from the trees planted by the Original Founder. There is a story of a man who died when the emperor's soldier hit him with a club, just because he was pleading the cause of a widow who was being mistreated."

"One of the faithful followers, who fed daily on the precious fruit, came over and touched this man on the shoulders after he had not been breathing for six hours. The follower then breathed on the man and commanded his spirit to return to his body. The man suddenly began to breathe and sat up with a strange look in his eyes, like he was confused. When he realized where he was, he told everyone that he had been in the most beautiful place, and he wished he could have stayed there."

Rule Keeper was also very excited about the fascinating information he was discovering in the scrolls. But every so often, he would groan within himself. If only he had read the scrolls in his youth! He would have had a totally different perspective on life, and many people would have been blessed by the knowledge that he was now taking in.

Patient Hope had not yet discovered the original name of the village, but what he had learned kept him going and excited to read more. Rule Keeper shared with him anything he thought might interest him, including a reference to the special well in the heart of the village. It seems the villagers were very dependent on that well. It was used to water the trees, and the water was also very good to drink. In fact, many of the residents would bottle some of the well water and take it into Normal Jungle to give others a drink. Those who accepted a drink of water from the well liked it so much that they usually left the jungle and moved to the village.

Patient Hope thanked Rule Keeper repeatedly for helping him and for making the scrolls available to him. "God is using you now in a most significant way to reverse the results of your past decisions. The good you accomplish through this will be more than you have ever imagined. You will become known as the 'Keeper of the Secret Scrolls', and you will be honored by truth-seekers everywhere."

DAY TWO

At the insistence of Rule Keeper, Patient Hope spent the night with him so as not to waste time walking home. They were both back up and at it early the next morning. Over and over they would stop and share with each other details of the original village that they had never known before.

By the end of the second day, the two very exhausted elders had learned many valuable bits of information, but they still had not solved the mystery of the original name of the village. They had just a few small scrolls left to read, so Patient Hope agreed to spend one more night with Rule Keeper.

THE NAME

DAY THREE

The next morning after a quick breakfast, Patient Hope carefully opened the smallest scroll, without a lot of expectation in his heart. As he looked at the heading at the top of the scroll, he was in shock. He almost dropped the scroll as his hands began to tremble. "I can't believe what I just read!" he stammered out loud.

"What is it?" shouted Rule Keeper. "What did you read?"

"The heading, I can't believe the heading of this scroll!"

"Well, what does it say? You're keeping me in suspense."

"It says," Patient Hope was now speaking slowly and deliberately, "it says, 'The One Hundredth Annual Official Census of MIRACLE FRUIT CITY'. Can you believe it? The village was a city and its name was Miracle Fruit. The name of the city was Miracle Fruit! I have read that they also ate vegetables, but they were famous for their fruit; not their veggies. And look here, the results of the census reveal that the city was much, much larger than Veggie Village."

"Wow…oh my goodness!" Rule Keeper was now pacing his living room floor. "It's no wonder that the founder of my district didn't want us to read these scrolls! He didn't believe in the fruit at all – only the various veggies. He told us the fruit was only given to get the village started, that we didn't need it anymore, and as long as we ate our veggies, we'd be okay. But look at how we have declined in population, while Normal Jungle has doubled and tripled. I think we need the fruit after all. Why would the Original Founder name the city 'Miracle Fruit' if He didn't want the fruit to last?"

The rest of the scroll gave names and addresses of all the residents of Miracle Fruit City. Patient Hope skimmed through the names out of curiosity. Near the bottom, he noticed a family named Dreamer. Under the family name there was a report of a brand new member of the Dreamer family. The baby's name was Fearless Dreamer. Patient Hope felt the presence of the Original Founder like the radiant warmth of the noon-day sun when he read that name, Fearless Dreamer. Inside his inner being, he heard a voice saying, "Don't forget that name!"

There was one more scroll for each of the elders to read. Rule Keeper opened his scroll with mixed emotions. Reading the scrolls had been quite an adventure, but his eyes were burning from so much reading, especially since some of the scrolls were difficult to read because of their age and the fading ink. He was somewhat relieved that this was the last scroll, but at the same time he was a bit disappointed that there would be no more new discoveries when these last two scrolls had been read.

He read the heading at the top of the scroll. "Oh my, look at this! Patient Hope, look, look! We've surely saved the best for the last. Look at this heading!"

MEETING MINUTES

Patient Hope scurried to look over the shoulder of Rule Keeper. There in bold hand printed letters were the words, "The Fate of the Fruit Trees Is Debated by City Elders."

"I think you might want to look at this first," said Rule Keeper. "I'll look at the other one."

"Thanks so much! This is like finding a huge jewel. How could you ever place a value on it?"

Spellbound, Patient Hope read line after line of the records of the city elders' meeting. The vast majority of the elders were of the opinion that the fruit trees were no longer producing enough fruit to justify the space they occupied in the city. Many pointed out that the vegetables produced in the citizens gardens and the perimeter fields were of excellent quality and very nutritious for the health and well-being of all the residents.

Suddenly, Patient Hope's jaw dropped. Once again he said, "I can't believe what I just read."

"What is it?"

"It says that the oldest of the elders was the only one to defend the fruit trees. He was the only one who voted to keep them alive. And his name – his name – was Fearless Dreamer. I just read his name in the census scroll. He was a newborn baby in that census. I was told in my spirit to remember that name. I didn't have to wait long to see it again."

Patient Hope read all the arguments of the elders who opposed keeping the trees. It seemed to him that many of the elders felt uncomfortable with the fact that people remembered the miracle power of the fruit trees from earlier days. Too many people had asked why they didn't see many miracles anymore and why the trees weren't producing the same quality of fruit that their ancestors had seen. The trees were too much of a reminder of what used to be. The elders were convinced that it must have been the will of the Original Founder for the fruit trees to die out, and the trees should not be allowed to take up valuable space.

Fearless Dreamer, on the other hand, challenged them to examine their hearts. He implied that the fruit had deteriorated because their love for the Original Founder had deteriorated. He made one statement that very much impressed Patient Hope. Fearless Dreamer was quoted as saying, "Love is the fruit of the heart which is devoted to the Original Founder. The state of the physical fruit is a reflection of the state of the spiritual fruit of our hearts."

The other younger elders resented his implications and argued vehemently that they were just as righteous as he was and they would not listen to him. The meeting ended with a decision to start cutting down the trees and using the wood for firewood during the cold winter season. The roots were to be pulled up and the ground would be tilled for the planting of more vegetables.

The final paragraph in the meeting minutes brought up the issue of the city's name. Clearly, the name was an embarrassment to the elders, and they suggested that everyone come up with a new name for the city at the next elder's meeting.

Meanwhile, Rule Keeper was reading the very last scroll. For the most part it was pretty repetitious, and he was about to roll up the scroll when the last few paragraphs caught his attention.

THE PROPHECY

What caught his weary eye was a prophecy by a Miracle Fruit City elder. He prophesied that the city would fade in significance and its influence would be weakened for many years. But some day, the Original Founder would raise up a new generation of truth-seekers who would discover the hidden and forgotten seeds, and the miracle fruit would be restored to the city again.

When Patient Hope read the prophecy, he dropped to his knees and gave thanks to the Original Founder who was certainly with them, orchestrating everything in such an amazing way. Rule Keeper, who had never been much of a worshipper, joined him on his knees and also gave thanks, tears streaming like rivers down his aged cheeks.

The two older gentlemen finally rose to their feet, and Patient Hope cleared his throat, visibly moved by the precious relationship that the Original Founder had brought them. Patient Hope knew he had to leave, but he was leaving differently than he had arrived. He had gained a dear and valuable friend and he knew that they would be together again.

"I hate to leave now," he said, "but I have some amazing young radicals that will be incredibly excited to hear what we have discovered together in these scrolls. They are waiting for me and I need to get back tonight. May the Original Founder continue to watch over you and keep you from all harm."

"And may He do the same for you, my brother! I will pray that we meet again soon."

Chapter Seven

The Well

It was almost dark when Patient Hope arrived back in his district of Veggie Village, and he went straight to the home of Extreme Courage. He found a few young radicals there seated around the kitchen table. They quickly stopped talking when Patient Hope arrived and then ran to the door excitedly, several of them talking at once.

"Whoa guys, it sounds like everyone is excited," remarked Patient Hope. "I have some exciting news, but it sounds like you have some too."

"We sure do," said Strong Support. "Quiet Meekness had a very amazing dream. Let her tell you about it."

"I can't wait to hear it", he replied, "and then I'll tell you what I've discovered over the past three days."

For the next two hours, the young radicals and the gentle elder exchanged their remarkable stories. They were all overwhelmed with the progress they had made so quickly, and they felt such an awareness of the greatness of the destiny they were living out. They also felt an overpowering love for one another and for the Original Founder who was truly watching over them and directing their steps.

After spending some time giving thanks to the Original Founder, the young radicals turned to Patient Hope, who cleared his throat and began to speak.

Preparing for a Great Adventure

"It's time now to prepare for the next important steps. Let's summarize what we know and what we don't yet know. First of all, we discovered the original name of our village. It was Miracle Fruit City, not Veggie Village. Obviously, the name was changed because it was no longer known for its miracle fruit, but rather for the vegetables it has been growing. The name was changed from "city" to "village" because it had decreased in population, as well as in its influence on Normal Jungle."

"We know there was an early city elder named Fearless Dreamer who opposed the destruction of the trees and wanted to preserve them. We don't know yet if any seeds were preserved, but if they were, chances are that Fearless Dreamer was the one who preserved them."

"We also believe that Quiet Meekness was given a dream concerning the source of the Living Water. She knows the exact spot where she found the well in her dream. Many of you have been preparing to go into the city and search for the well. I agree that we must find that well, but we need to review our strategy and ask the Original Founder to help us with this endeavor."

Extreme Courage interjected, "We have been gathering a lot of tools and ropes to uncover and examine the well. We want to lower a bucket into the well to see if we can bring up some water. We are so excited that we can hardly contain ourselves. We have been waiting for your return, because we didn't want to do anything until we had your approval."

"That was wise of you, Extreme Courage. We're at a very critical stage in the process. We can no longer stay out of sight talking, reading and planning. It's time for action, we will have to expose ourselves in the heart of Veggie Village and we do risk the danger of being discovered."

"Some of the village elders have a very aggressive and anti-restoration attitude. They are very content with their traditions and the status-quo, and they are ready to fight anyone who advocates change. Fortunately,

Rule Keeper has had a change of heart. He was one of the most antagonistic of all, but that makes only two of us among the dozens of elders."

"We must be extremely careful. If we blow our cover, and they find out what we are doing, they may impose harsh punishment on all of us. Then it would become very difficult for us to proceed."

"You are very wise, Patient Hope," declared Extreme Courage. "We need your wisdom more now than ever. I'd like to go over our plans so far and you can tell us if you think we are on the right track."

"We have created a map of the region, and we plan to position eight lookouts, with two at every approach to the well site. The lookouts will use the call of a night owl to signal those working out in the open, if they see anyone coming. They have been practicing those calls for several days already, and they actually have it down very well. They actually fooled me the other night. If we hear the owl hoot, then we will quickly hide in the bushes at the southeast corner of the intersection."

"We will arrive at precisely five hours after sunset. The moon will have set by that time, and we will work only by star light if the sky is clear. If it's cloudy, we will use small candles with shields to keep others from seeing them."

"I will accompany two strong young men with tools to dig up and lift the lid off of the well. When we get the lid off, we will lower a bucket into the well by rope. We will then be able to see how deep the well is and if there is still any water down there. If we discover water, we will test it in various ways to see if it still has any extraordinary powers, and then we will be ready for the seeds. I sure wish we had a better idea of where to find those seeds."

Patient Hope responded, "Of course, Extreme Courage, don't we all? But it sounds like you have made some very thorough plans. I would suggest one little bit of strategy to avoid making unnecessary noise. The well lid is probably made of heavy metal, as are the tools that will be used to pry it up. Whenever metal meets metal, it is very difficult to keep it quiet. I advise you to bring some pieces of cloth to cover your metal tools when you try to pry up the well cover. It may be extremely heavy as well, and you should have two or three more young men ready to help you lift it and move it."

"As always, you think of things we would have missed, and those things could be critical to our success," remarked Extreme Courage. "Thank you so much for that advice."

"My pleasure!" beamed Patient Hope. "I'm sure we'll think of a few more things before we try to pull this off.

"How soon can we do this?" asked Extreme Courage.

"I would wait three more days," said Patient Hope. "That will give us time to prepare and for me to do a little more important research while you go over your plans."

The three days passed quickly and everyone worked hard preparing for the big night of adventure. They would soon take their first big risk of trying to uncover a well that had been covered for many centuries. What were the chances that they would actually find it? What were the chances that they would find water in such an ancient well? And what were the chances that the water would actually have special qualities? The young radicals had difficulty sleeping those three nights before the big event.

Patient Hope slept only a few hours every night, and he spent those extra hours staying up late reading and rereading the scrolls that were available to him. He had not borrowed any new scrolls the last three days, out of concern that someone might get too curious, and he would have to answer unnecessary questions. He contented himself with a scrupulous review of the scrolls in his possession, hoping to find something he had overlooked.

Nothing really leapt out of the scrolls at him, but the more he read, the more peace he felt about their project. He did ask the Original Founder a few questions and listened patiently, hoping he would hear some answers.

One question he asked was, "Shouldn't we be looking for the seeds first, before finding the water? It seems like the water won't really do a lot of good until we find the seeds." Then he remembered the words of Gentle Compassion, regarding the importance of the Living Water. He decided to leave the problem of the missing seeds in the hands of the Original Founder, who surely knew what He was doing.

THE ADVENTURE BEGINS

The big night finally arrived, and the young radicals met at the tool shed three hours after sunset to coordinate the timing of their activities. They were grateful for a cloudless, starlit night. After one hour, they began to slip out into the darkness, choosing different paths to arrive at the same destination.

The journey on foot took almost an hour from the tool shed. The eight lookouts arrived at their stations first. Softly, they confirmed their locations with muffled hoots. They were all in their stations thirty minutes or so before the hour of destiny. They all wore warm, dark clothing and huddled in the cool night air waiting for Extreme Courage and his young companions.

Finally, Extreme Courage, Strong Support and five other strong young men arrived at the designated location. They were accompanied by Quiet Meekness, so she could show them the exact location that she had seen in her dream. Before venturing out into the street, they stopped to confer in the darkness with one of the lookouts.

"Have you seen anything moving at all?" Extreme Courage asked the lookout.

"Not a thing!" he replied.

"Okay, team, are we ready?" Extreme Courage asked in a loud whisper.

"We are ready!" they whispered back.

"Quiet Meekness, please lead the way, and may the Original Founder watch over us tonight."

With quiet confidence, Quiet Meekness led Extreme Courage, Strong Support and two of the others, who were carrying picks and shovels, into the street. The rest of the team waited with the lookout ready for action should they be needed. The dream of Quiet Meekness came alive again, as she walked into the hard-packed dirt street. She came to the place that felt exactly right and dragged her foot on the ground to see if it would catch on anything. The roads in Veggie Village were never paved, just repaired with dirt and gravel when potholes occurred. She hoped the lid was sticking up a little like it had in her dream.

Quiet Meekness felt a little bump with her foot and checked it out. It was just a large piece of gravel. She tried again and it was another little rock. She tried again and there was nothing at all. For five minutes or so, she moved around the area and kept feeling with her foot, wondering why she wasn't finding the lid like she had in the dream. Everything felt so right, but she wasn't finding the well.

The young men with the shovels and picks began to quietly poke around to see if they could find anything interesting. There was nothing to find but normal dirt and gravel. Tears began to flow from the cheeks of Quiet Meekness as frustration and discouragement began to overcome her sensitive spirit.

She had caused this entire adventure. What if her dream was not from the Original Founder, but just a figment of her imagination? How embarrassing it would be if nothing resulted from all this effort! Her heart was growing heavier and heavier.

Strong Support sensed her frustration and came quickly to her side. "Don't get discouraged," he exhorted, "we're going to find it. Remember, we've always had to demonstrate tenacity and faith before any breakthrough occurred. You didn't get that dream the first night. We all had to wait patiently. Now where is the spot you checked out first?"

Quiet Meekness was immediately encouraged and grateful to Strong Support for his sensitive spirit.

"Right over here," she replied, wiping her tears and poking at the spot where she removed the first rock."

"Let me dig a little," Strong Support said as he began to dig quietly in the exact spot. His first efforts produced nothing, but the ground was a little softer than in other spots. He decided to drive the shovel harder and deeper into the ground than before.

Suddenly, there was a sound of metal on metal. Patient Hope had been right; it made a loud noise. Everyone paused and looked around to see if the noise had been heard by anyone in the neighborhood, but it appeared that no one had woken up. The three young men and Quiet Meekness took a closer look. The other shovels moved a little more dirt and then by the light of a small candle, they took a closer look at the metal object which Strong Support had uncovered. It sure looked like it could be the metal lid to a well.

Extreme Courage waved to the four waiting young radicals to join them with their tools. They quickly began to dig in a wide circle until they uncovered the circumference of a large metal lid. It was a circle about six feet in diameter. They worked quickly and quietly, energized by a surge of adrenalin. It was the middle of the night, but sleep was now the farthest thing from their minds. Every one of them was intensely focused on finding the Living Water.

The lookouts gazed from their posts in the darkness at what was happening in the middle of the street. They were so curious that they sometimes forgot to look around and check for trouble. So far everything was going ahead like clockwork. The digging crew had found the well, they had located the edge of the lid, and they were now busy clearing off the hard-packed dirt and gravel.

The whole crew was anxious to get the lid off. Just a few more minutes and they should be able to pry the lid up and slide it off the ancient well. It was their personal treasure, and they yearned to taste that ancient Living Water that the Original Founder had talked so frequently about.

The lid was about ninety percent cleared off when Extreme Courage and his courageous crew heard the clear sound of a night owl. Shocked out of their euphoria, they looked at one another in the darkness and whispered, "Head for the bushes!"

Clutching their tools, they scurried into the nearby shrubbery according to their thoroughly rehearsed plan. Quietly, Extreme Courage crawled over to the nearest lookout and whispered, "Did you see anything?"

"No, I didn't see anything, but I heard the night owl cry."

"Well, I guess it was one of the other lookouts," said Extreme Courage.

Everyone waited in the still night air for about fifteen minutes, and then suddenly they saw it. Heading in their direction, flapping its wings silently and hooting as it flew, was a big old night owl.

"Can you believe it?" whispered Extreme Courage. "It was a real night owl! Let's get back to work. We are so close now. It would have been such a disaster if we had been discovered and forced to quit now that we are on the threshold of such a great discovery. Let's get the lid off of that well."

Working quickly, the young radicals finished the task of cleaning off the heavy dirt and gravel from the heavy lid. Next they grabbed their metal picks and rods and placed the sharp ends into the crack around the lid. As they began to pry up the lid, it began to move, and the rubbing action of the metal on metal once again created a rather loud noise. In their excitement to get the lid off, they had temporarily forgotten the advice of Patient Hope.

Extreme Courage looked around cautiously again to make sure no one in the neighborhood had been awakened by the noise. Then he reached inside his garments and pulled out several pieces of cloth, which he had brought for the occasion and distributed them to his friends. They placed them on the sharp end of their tools and the difference was noticed immediately.

Stationed around the lid, each one pried as hard as he could. The lid moved, but they were not able to raise it even an inch. After a few minutes of work, Extreme Courage suggested a different strategy.

"Let's all work on the same side of the lid and see if we can get something under it."

The strategy worked and soon they had a metal bar between the lid and the edge of the well. They moved a third of the way around the lid and repeated the process. Finally, they were able to get the full circle of the lid raised off the wall of the well.

They could tell that this lid was incredibly heavy and they were thankful for the wise advice that Patient Hope had given them. It appeared to be at least two inches thick, probably made of cast iron. Whoever had placed the lid on the well must have wanted it to be there forever. They just hoped they had enough young men for the job.

Extreme Courage decided to bring in two of his lookouts, as well as the extra young men he had brought with him, to make moving the lid an easier task. At the same time, he knew that they had to be careful so none of them would fall into the well. They would need to know which direction they were going and how to avoid walking right into the hole.

The lid removal operation turned out to be a great success. The young radicals had just enough strength to lift it and carry it sideways without losing any of their number into the well.

"Wonderful! Excellent work guys!" exhorted Extreme Courage under his breath. "Now before we lower the bucket into the well, let's drop a small stone and see if we can hear it splash in the water."

The whole crew listened eagerly as Extreme Courage dropped a rock about the size of a small egg. The first sound was more like a thud, followed by a series of thuds, like the rock was bouncing off the wall of the well. Finally, there was a slightly different and very faint-sounding noise and then nothing. Only the sharpest ears heard the final sound, and it was such a weak sound that no one was sure if it was the sound of water or more rocks at the bottom.

"Well team, I don't think that told us a lot, except that the walls of the well may not be as straight as we expected. Let's try the bucket."

Quickly they attached the bucket to the long rope and began to lower it. It wasn't long until the rope went slack. The bucket was hung up on something and it didn't appear to be water.

Backup Plan

We're going to have to send Strong Support in to find out what's happening. Let's get the big heavy rope out of the bushes." Extreme Courage knew they had to work quickly. Getting the lid off had taken longer than they had expected, especially with the false alarm caused by the night owl.

They quickly adjusted to Plan B, which was lowering Strong Support into the well. The young men took their posts, as they had carefully rehearsed the past few days. The rope was prepared with two loops for Strong Support's feet. Extreme courage and four others held the rope as their privileged friend was slowly but surely lowered into the mouth of the well. In his right hand, Strong Support held onto a specially prepared candle holder designed to protect the flame from wind drafts and falling objects, such as dirt and rock. His left hand clung tightly to the rope.

Quiet Meekness leaned over the well and whispered to Strong Support, "May the Original Founder help you find the Living Water."

Lower and lower, the brave young radical descended into the ancient well, hoping and praying that he would be the first to find the water that had given life to the miracle fruit. Up above, Extreme Courage was counting the little knots they had tied every ten feet in the rope to measure how far down Strong Support was going. "That's thirty feet," he spoke softly to his team.

Once again, the rope went slack. "What's happening?" shouted Extreme Courage into the Well.

"The walls have narrowed suddenly and the hole is very small right here," replied Strong Support. "There is a big rocky ledge protruding into the hole on both sides of the well. I'll try to get down past it."

His voice was somewhat muffled, but the crew above was able to understand. They waited anxiously at the rim of the well, listening to the grunts and groans of Strong Support as he tried to squeeze his big muscular body through a very narrow space. Finally, he realized it just wasn't going to work. Very reluctantly, he asked Extreme Courage to pull him back up.

Back at the surface, Strong Support huddled with Extreme Courage and the others. "If I could have just gotten past that one spot, I may have been able to get all the way to the water, if there is any water down there."

Surprise Volunteer

"Let me go down!"

Everyone looked in the direction of that soft, sweet voice. It was Quiet Meekness. She was very petite and obviously very brave. "It may be our only chance and I want to do it," she insisted.

"We don't have many options at this time, and it's getting late," Extreme Courage reasoned. "The first light of dawn can't be too far away. If you are willing, we will let you down into the well."

"I'm very willing and anxious to do it as quickly as possible," Quiet Meekness replied.

Strong Support came to her side again, "Thank you for your courage. We'll be praying for you. And please take the smaller bucket; the big one might be too wide to fit through the opening."

The crew quickly put her feet in the rope stirrups; the special candle was placed in her hand and they lowered her down. When she reached the narrow part of the well, she discovered that it was a very tight squeeze, even for her slender frame, but with a little twisting and turning, she was able to get herself and the small bucket past the protruding rock formations.

Lower and lower Quiet Meekness descended into the deep well. Suddenly, she dislodged an object on a small rocky ledge with her feet. About two seconds later, she heard the object bounce off another ledge and then she heard a loud "Kersplash". Her heart leapt inside her chest. The well wasn't dry! The Living Water was still available!

"There's water down here!" she yelled upward.

Her voice was faint and muffled to the listening ears at the top of the well.

"Say that again, slowly," shouted Extreme Courage into the well, risking the chance of being heard by any early risers.

"THERE . . . IS . . . WATER . . . DOWN . . . HERE!" Quiet Meekness repeated as loud as she could.

"WONDERFUL! SHAKE THE ROPE WHEN YOU GET SOME IN THE BUCKET!"

Chapter Eight

The Surprise

It wasn't long before Quiet Meekness touched water with her feet. She felt the thrill of that touch go through her entire slender body. Quickly, she dipped the bucket, which had been tied to her waist. A little water splashed on her wrist. It felt very cool and soothing and it almost seemed to be alive.

Quiet Meekness shook the rope, hoping that they could feel the vibration at the top. At first there was no response, so she did it again as vigorously as she could, and shouted, "Now!" at the same time.

The eager young radicals got the message this time, and they began to pull up the brave little explorer. She was once again able to slip through the tight spot that had caused Strong Support to give up his attempt to get to the Living Water. Her biggest concern was that she didn't want to lose any of the precious treasure in the bucket. It seemed like it was taking forever to those above, but Quiet Meekness finally appeared at the mouth of the well with both the candle and the bucket handle in her left hand.

The first light of dawn was just beginning to illuminate the eastern horizon. Quiet Meekness was lifted safely out of the well with her extremely valuable cargo. Extreme Courage reached out and gently took the bucket and candle out of her hand. Shining the candle light directly into the bucket, he noticed a dark object floating in the bucket.

The Mysterious Object

"What's this?" questioned Extreme Courage.

Everyone looked intently at the round earthen vessel bobbing around in the water. It was clearly a man-made object. In the darkness, it had blended in with the water, and Quiet Meekness had not even noticed it. Now she stared at it in awe and disbelief. This must have been the object that her foot had dislodged on her way down to the water. Her heart was filled with an unusual excitement. Could this be what she was thinking it could be?

Extreme Courage's voice interrupted her inner thoughts, "Quiet Meekness, please take this bucket with you and go hide with the lookout in the bushes, while we close and cover up the well."

It was getting a bit lighter already, and the fearless crew once again lifted the well lid enough to place it over the six-foot hole. They quickly covered the lid with the loose rock and dirt and began to pack it down as hard as possible by hitting it as quietly as possible with the backs of their shovels and stomping on it with their feet.

"I think that will do it," said Extreme Courage. "Let's head back to the tool shed and take a better look at the water and the floating object."

Another Dream

Just then, they heard it again. It was the sound of a night owl, hooting softly. Then they heard the hooting again coming from another direction. Extreme Courage whispered loudly, "Head for the bushes!" He knew it was best to play it safe, even though he knew it could be another false alarm.

From the safety of the shrubs, they questioned their lookout. "Did you see something?"

"Yes, there's a man walking toward us," he whispered nervously.

THE SURPRISE

Sure enough, in the early dawn glow they could see a short, elderly man walking slowly towards the spot where they had been working only moments before. Transfixed, they watched the gentleman trudge deliberately down the road until he had reached the exact spot where the well was.

With reverence, the man knelt down on top of the well and bowed his head silently for about ten minutes. Suddenly, he began to move his hands in the dirt and appeared to get quite excited. He looked up and around quickly, wondering if he was being watched. He dug a little deeper with his hands and soon his fingers had touched the metal lid of the well.

Watching from the bushes, the young radicals could see that the elderly man was visibly shaken by his discovery. He quickly covered up the lid and patted the dirt and rocks down with his hands. Then he got up and stomped on it a little. Dusting off his hands, he headed back in the direction he had come from. This time Extreme Courage could see him a little better. Suddenly, he recognized him. He had seen him a few times before at Veggie Village functions.

His name was Devoted Worshipper. He was not a village elder, although no one seemed to know why. He was clearly one of the oldest men in the village and respected by the people, but not highly honored by the elders.

"Strong Support," whispered Extreme Courage, "I have another assignment for you. I'm sure you can complete this one. Please follow that man to see where he lives. We'll come back later and talk to him. The rest of us will slip back to the tool shed."

"At your service! You can count on me," said Strong Support.

As he promised, Strong Support followed Devoted Worshipper from a distance in the mid-dawn light. The others headed back with the bucket and its precious contents.

Safely in the old tool shed, the young radicals took a closer look at the spoils of their all-night adventure. The water was clear and sparkling.

It seemed to be dancing as a partner with the flickering light of the candles used to illuminate the shed.

WHAT IS IT?

And then there was that strange object, which was light enough to float in the water, but unlike anything they had ever seen before. Extreme Courage had taken it out of the water and carried it all the way back to the shed. He instinctively knew that it was important, and he wanted to make sure it would not be lost or harmed in any way. When he had first pulled the object out of the water and dried it off, he shook it gently. He was surprised to hear a very faint sound that told him there was something loose inside the hollow object.

As he examined the object more closely, he could tell that it was a container made of two pieces of pottery that had been sealed together with some kind of pitch. He scanned the tool shed for the appropriate instrument to perform the necessary surgical procedure on the mystery object. He finally spotted a small, sharp tool with a saw-toothed blade. He was reaching to pick it up when the tool shed door creaked open.

It was Patient Hope. He had chosen to stay home that night, allowing the young radicals to enjoy their adventure without any supervision from him. He wasn't quite up to the all-night activities at his age either. He did have faith that there would be some kind of success from the adventure, and he couldn't wait to find out what had happened.

The young radicals were all very excited to see him. Everyone started talking at once, but when Patient Hope put up his hand, they all quieted down. "It sounds like you youngsters are pretty excited," he said, grinning from ear to ear. "Gentle Compassion, you're a great story teller. Why don't you tell me what happened?"

Gentle Compassion had been in the bushes as one of the lookouts, but she was very aware of what had happened and began to recount the exciting events of the night. Then she began explaining how the old man, Devoted Worshipper, had kneeled on the exact spot where they had found the well.

At that point, Patient Hope interrupted her excitedly. "I've always known that there was something different about that man! He's always been shunned and isolated by the other elders. He's very much a loner, and since he lives so far away, I've never spent any time with him, but I always sensed he knew something that I didn't."

"I asked Strong Support to find out where he lives and report back," interjected Extreme Courage. "He should be here any time now."

Just then the door opened again and Strong Support walked in. "Mission accomplished," he declared.

"Awesome!" responded Extreme Courage. "We're all back together again, so now we can all witness the opening of the mysterious object that Quiet Meekness dislodged from the little ledge in the well wall. I found a tool that just might open it up."

Everyone leaned in to get a good look as Extreme Courage placed the object on the workbench and proceeded to work on cutting through the ancient sealant. Slowly but surely, he began to penetrate through the hardened pitch, which was now more like rock than pitch. After several minutes, the little tool had gotten through the sealant. Before long, the two halves were opened, exposing the treasure inside.

And there in front of their bulging eyes was the greatest treasure that they could ever have imagined finding. In perfect condition, like the day they had been placed in the container, were dozens of individual seeds, such as the Veggie Village inhabitants had never seen.

"Oh my goodness!" they all gasped in unison.

"This is and will always be a day to remember," responded Patient Hope solemnly. "Let's stop and give thanks to the Original Founder for helping us discover these precious seeds and the Living Water at the same time. Now I know why He didn't answer my question about going for the Living Water before we had the seeds. He knew we would find the seeds when we searched for the Living Water. I think He is saying what Gentle Compassion stated earlier, that the Living Water is the greater thing and is also the source of the fruit that will be produced. Without the Living Water, the fruit would have no power."

Giving Thanks

The whole crew then bowed their heads in reverence and gave thanks to the Original Founder, Who had guided their adventure and helped them keep it a secret. They also thanked Him for speaking to Fearless Dreamer about preserving the precious seeds and placing them on that little rocky ledge in the well. Most of the young radicals had tears streaming down their faces, and Patient Hope was weeping unashamedly, knowing that his life-long search had finally come to fruition.

After about fifteen minutes of giving thanks, Patient Hope spoke up again. "Now that we have the sacred seeds, we need to make some plans for growing the fruit trees. I suggest we waste no time in getting started. Why don't we sort the seeds to see how many kinds of seed we have and how many of each kind. Then we can soak some of the seeds overnight in the Living Water. When they have sprouted, we can plant them in clay pots and then divide them amongst ourselves to keep them more inconspicuous. We don't want to raise any more suspicion than necessary."

"Let's get started. Most of you have a full day's work ahead of you without any sleep. I don't exactly know how you youngsters can do it. I'm getting tired just thinking about it."

As the young radicals began to divide the seeds into categories, they discovered that there were nine different types of seeds. Fearless Dreamer had saved five of each of them – forty-five seeds in all.

Patient Hope added, "Let's start with two of each kind today and soak them in a little water. We'll hide them under this old bucket in the back corner and check back on them tonight."

"Extreme Courage, you can take the remaining seeds in the container back to your house and keep them hidden until we decide to plant them as well. I'm sure we'll learn some things from these first two seeds that will help us with the last three seeds of each kind."

Most of the young radicals had to work all day harvesting vegetables, but their minds were not on vegetables, but rather on the miracle fruit they were preparing to produce. They all wondered how long it would be before they could actually eat the fruit produced from those forty-five seeds. Adrenalin kept them going during the day, and they couldn't wait to get back to the tool shed to see if anything was happening to the seeds that were soaking in the Living Water.

Devoted Worshipper

Meanwhile, Strong Support and Extreme Courage, who were both excused from the fields that day, accompanied Patient Hope to the house of Devoted Worshipper, the old gentleman who had knelt on top of the well. Strong Support knocked on the old man's door, and they all waited patiently to see if he would come to the door.

Finally, they heard the slow shuffle of feet and then a faint voice, "Who's there?"

"It's me, Patient Hope, and a couple of young friends. Please let us in. We need to talk to you."

"Alright, I'll be right with you."

After another minute or two the door finally opened. "Come on in. What can I do for you, my friends?"

The three of them entered and sat down. They could quickly tell that Devoted Worshipper didn't have a lot of company. They realized that the delay in answering the door was because he had been trying to clear a place for them to sit. There were stacks of scrolls on the table and floor, some of which had obviously covered the now empty chairs. One thing was very clear, Devoted Worshipper liked to read.

"Let's get right to the point," said Patient Hope to one of the few men older than himself in Veggie Village. "These young men saw you kneeling on the ancient well site this morning."

"They did?" Devoted Worshipper reacted with a mixture of shock and fear. "You know about the well? Who told you? Were you the ones who dug up the dirt?"

The visitors proceeded to tell him the whole story and Devoted Worshipper began to weep softly. "I can't believe after all these years that the Original Founder has chosen to answer all of our prayers. I have been praying for this since I was nineteen, when I first became interested in the miracle fruit."

"The village elders were very angry with me then, and because I wouldn't stop questioning them, they vowed that I would never become a village elder, no matter how long I lived. They passed their judgment along to all of the elders who followed them, and I have been shunned and isolated all of my life. No one would give their daughter to me in marriage, so I have lived a long lonely life."

"But the Original Founder became very precious to me and He has taught me many things. He showed me where to find these hidden scrolls that no one else knew about. I learned to read them and discovered many secrets. One secret was the location of the ancient well. Since then, I have gone to the spot before daylight every day that I could, and I prayed to the Original Founder asking Him to restore the Living Water and the miracle fruit. I've done this for a few years now and no one has ever seen me, as far as I know, until this day. I can hardly believe that you found the water and the seeds at the same time."

Extreme Courage remarked, "I've been wondering how Fearless Dreamer got down into the well all by himself."

"Well, that would have been quite a feat for sure," replied Devoted Worshipper, "but he wasn't alone. He had a son and three grandsons that believed his story. The youngest was about fourteen years old and quite slender, and he helped him put the seeds on that lower ledge, close to the water."

"One of the scrolls, which I have hidden under my bed, was written by Fearless Dreamer and was buried in a field. The Original Founder told me in a dream where to find it. It was one of the most exciting days of my life, when I found that scroll, but I was never allowed to share it with anyone. I know now that I can share it with you."

After some more excited conversation, the happy trio excused themselves and headed home. "What an amazing day!" Extreme Courage declared.

The others totally agreed with him; the last twenty-four hours had been intense and fruitful. Of course, they didn't have any fruit yet – just some ancient seeds. They still had no proof that the seeds would sprout, but they were extremely hopeful, given the events of the past day.

For all the young radicals still laboring in the fields, their work day had finally come to an end. After their evening meal, at the appointed time, they slipped out to the old tool shed. Once again, they were not disappointed.

Growing Seeds

The container with the seeds was retrieved from under the old bucket and quickly examined by the eager young radicals and Patient Hope. Incredibly, each seed had grown a sprout of over half an inch in the past twelve hours or so.

"My, oh my, they're ready for potting already," said Patient Hope. "These are not normal seeds, my young friends. At this rate, we're going to have to find places to plant them in the open very soon, and we better scout out the best sites. We may have to face some angry village elders before too long. We must be ready for the negative consequences of our labors, but I know the Original Founder is still with us and He will help us."

Chapter Nine

THE ATTACK

The young radicals quickly potted the eighteen tender sprouts and then went home to get a good night's rest. They had been awake a long time, and they were totally exhausted by now, but incredibly happy.

POTENTIAL DANGERS

While the young radicals were catching up on their lost sleep, Patient Hope was meditating on the events of the past two days and their potential consequences. He knew some things that he had never shared with the young radicals. In some of the scrolls, there were stories of serious violence against the young radicals of previous generations. There had been Veggie Village Elders who had been cruel and vindictive to anyone whom they perceived was challenging their spiritual authority by suggesting the restoration of the original fruit.

There had been village trials in which the elders had imposed severe punishment for such obvious rebellion. There had even been times when young radicals had been burned at the stake or beheaded because they refused to change their minds about the miracle fruit. Others had been imprisoned for life and died without ever seeing their dreams come to fruition.

Patient Hope knew that some of the current elders were capable of very harsh measures if their authority was challenged. Rule Keeper had been one of the toughest, and Patient Hope was extremely thankful to the Original Founder for the change that had come to his heart. However, there were several elders who were very much like Rule Keeper had been prior to the dream that changed him forever, and Patient Hope knew that a nasty confrontation was a very likely possibility.

In addition, according to some of the scrolls, there had been frequent trouble from the Normal Jungle residents when the young radicals gained momentum in their push to restore the miracle fruit to Veggie Village. It seemed that by some spiritual power, the most wicked jungle residents knew that something was going on and they would get extremely agitated.

The records showed that some of them would invade the community during the night and steal or destroy their crops and throw rocks at the simple houses the Veggie Village people lived in. Over the years, many had been injured and a few had even been killed when they tried to resist the invaders. Of course, there was no logical reason for the attacks, but it seemed that whatever went on in Veggie Village was somehow affecting the attitudes of those living in Normal Jungle.

Things had been quiet so far. The Normal Jungle residents had been keeping their distance from Veggie Village. It seemed that they feared getting too close to the strange folk living out in the hot sun. It had also been some time since the Veggie Village residents had visited the jungle to share their beliefs with its inhabitants.

As Patient Hope pondered these things, he whispered a prayer to the Original Founder and asked for more wisdom and strategy. The way the sprouts were growing, the trees would grow quickly. Where could they plant them without them being discovered and destroyed?

Not only that, they would need to get more Living Water from the well to water the plants. The one small bucket of Living Water would quickly be used up, and they didn't want to risk using the regular water from the other village wells on their precious fruit trees. Patient Hope was also well aware of the fact that the more often they uncovered the well, the more likely they were to be discovered.

Perhaps he should call a special meeting with the other village elders. Maybe he could get a majority of them to listen to him and the fruit trees would be protected. However, the chances of that were pretty slim and he knew it.

Patient Hope finally drifted off to sleep, although he had not yet come up with any answers to his many questions. He had waited all his life for this moment and now that it had finally come, he knew that he was not prepared. But he also had confidence that the Original Founder would not have brought them this far to let them lose the precious fruit that they were so close to producing.

By early the next morning before the work day began, the young radicals and Patient Hope met at the tool shed. The sprouts had already grown up through the soil, and little green shoots were reaching towards the sun. They all looked at each other with both excitement and bewilderment on their faces. It was amazing and wonderful, but what would they do next? Where would they transplant their amazing treasures?

They all committed to a day of asking the Original Founder for wisdom and strategy, knowing that decisions would have to be made quickly. Extreme Courage suggested that two of them should sleep that night in the tool shed to make sure that the little trees would be safe.

By evening, the plants had grown about three inches tall. A small cupful of Living Water was poured into each of the pots to keep the soil as moist as possible throughout the coming heat of the day. The small bucket of Living Water was now almost empty and the plants would require more water as they grew larger and sent their roots down deeper.

THE NIGHT WATCH

Extreme Courage and Strong Support volunteered to take the first night watch with the little trees. While Strong Support rested on the hard dirt floor, Extreme Courage sat up on an old bucket and prayed to the Original

Founder. After about three hours had passed, they changed positions.

Approximately ten minutes after Extreme Courage lay down to sleep, Strong Support heard an unusual sound, and then he heard men's voices speaking in muffled tones. He sat up quietly and looked out a window. In the dim starlight, he could make out the silhouettes of five or six young men with long objects that appeared to be sticks or swords in their hands. They were walking out into the middle of the broccoli field. They had obviously come from Normal Jungle and they were up to no good.

Strong Support quietly roused Extreme Courage out of a deep sleep. Together they watched as the men began to spread out in the field. Then, at a signal from their leader, they began to whack away at the ripening broccoli crop. The two young radicals looked at each other for a moment, and then they looked around the shed in the dim light and found some metal tools that could be used to make a loud noise.

Should they or shouldn't they? That was the question. Should they let the wild jungle dwellers destroy their broccoli crop, or should they try to scare them away and risk being discovered, along with the precious fruit trees? They knew they could be turned on and personally attacked, and they also knew that they could be laying their lives on the line and possibly the future of the miracle fruit.

Extreme Courage breathed a hurried but heart-felt prayer to the Original Founder and made his decision. He could not allow the labor of so many village friends to be destroyed in a few moments. He had to do something.

Slipping out into the darkness and hiding behind the shed, the two of them banged their tools furiously on the side of the metal shed, making as big a racket as possible. The jungle dwellers were instantly spooked and ran as fast as their legs could carry them back into the safety of their jungle.

Watching them run in sheer panic brought a smile to the faces of the two brave young radicals. Their secret was still safe and the damage to the broccoli field was not nearly as severe as it could have been.

But what had prompted the attack in the first place? Nothing like this had happened for some time. Something was agitating the nearby tribe, and who knew what would happen next?

The night watch continued with nothing else disturbing their rest. By morning, some of the young radicals showed up again, along with Patient Hope. The potted plants had grown significantly again during the night, and hiding them was going to become a huge problem within a day or two if things continued as they were.

There were now many more questions than answers, but everyone had an assignment for the day and they left the potted plants as hidden as possible. Extreme Courage and Patient Hope waited until everyone else had gone, and they began to walk slowly away from the tool shed together. They wanted to talk and also to inspect the damage done to the broccoli plants.

Assessing the Damage

The broccoli plants had suffered a fair amount of damage, but it was not visible from a distance. It would probably be several days before anyone inspected that part of the field. Harvest could begin in another ten days or so, but hopefully, no one would notice until then. Most Veggie Village residents were busy harvesting other crops in their various districts.

The two men began to discuss the few available options. None of the options made a lot of sense and they were both feeling a little frustrated. They knew they were on a miraculous journey, but without another quick miracle, their labor could be all in vain.

They had been walking and talking with their heads down to keep their voices from carrying too far, when suddenly they heard the voices of strangers. Standing a few yards away, shielding their eyes in the bright morning sun, were two men from the jungle. Judging by their attire, they were obviously from a fairly primitive tribe.

"Hello," said the older man, "we must talk with someone."

Patient Hope and Extreme Courage looked at each other, then at the two strangers. "What can we do for you?" responded Patient Hope.

"Last night we came to your field to destroy your crop because our tribe has lost many children to a terrible disease. The children cry from pain, hold their stomachs and then they suddenly die. Our witch doctor said that the people from Veggie Village were putting a curse on us, and he told us to take revenge by attacking and destroying your vegetable garden."

"We had just started to destroy your crop when we heard a loud noise like the sound of a big army coming. We were very afraid, so we ran back into the jungle. We talked to our witch doctor again, and he told us that your gods must be stronger than our gods. We were told that we must return and ask forgiveness from you and your gods, so that the curse will be taken off of our children. We have come today to ask what we must do to make the curse leave our children."

Patient Hope suddenly felt the strong presence of the Original Founder very close to him. His heart was filled with compassion for the poor jungle dwellers, and he sensed that he was being given wisdom from outside of himself. He turned to the two men and said, "Let us consult for a minute."

After a few minutes of discussion, Patient Hope and Extreme Courage nodded their heads in agreement and then turned their attention back to the waiting jungle dwellers. "We have an answer for you. You have done the right thing in coming to us. We forgive you for trying to destroy our crop, and we will ask the Great Spirit of the Original Founder of our village to stop the curse on your children. We did not curse you, but perhaps another tribe did."

THE STRATEGY

"Our Original Founder can make the curse go away, but you must cooperate with us. The Great Spirit of the Original Founder of this village has visited us, and he instructed us to grow special fruit trees. If properly watered and cared for, these trees will produce special fruit that have miracle power. We believe they will even heal your children."

"We must keep these trees a secret from some of our villagers who do not believe in their power. We need a safe place to grow these trees. If you will clear a stretch of the jungle between our broccoli field and where you live, we will come and plant eighteen special fruit trees. If you clear the land and then help us guard and protect these trees from harm, we will allow you to eat this fruit, and you and your children will become strong and healthy. You will also be allowed to become a follower of our Original Founder. When the trees are grown and produce fruit with seeds, we can plant more trees, and you can live under the shade of these special trees, which will grow large and strong."

Patient Hope paused and then added, "You must make your decision today and begin clearing some jungle land immediately. We must plant these trees within three days."

The two jungle dwellers conferred for a few moments and then the older one spoke, "We will do as you ask. Our women are very angry at us because our children are dying. Everyone is sad and angry and the witch doctor said we must do whatever you ask. We will begin to cut and clear some land between your field and our homes. We will have it ready for you to plant your trees in three days. We will put guards around the trees day and night. We can also eat some of the fruit when it grows, yes?"

"You can certainly eat the fruit," responded Patient Hope, "but you must save the seeds and clear more land and plant them in your jungle."

"We also promise that, as you request," came the quick reply. "We will return in two days and show you where we are clearing the land. Be here again this time in two days."

"We will be here," Patient Hope replied.

The jungle dwellers bowed low and backed off, quickly disappearing into the vast jungle. Patient Hope and Extreme Courage shook their heads in amazement.

Extreme Courage said, "I know the Original Founder has been with us. If I had not decided to bang those tools on the tool shed, then we would never have had this breakthrough. Our crop would have been destroyed, which would have brought out all of the village elders, and they probably would have discovered our potted trees."

"Yes, my young friend, the Original Founder was certainly guiding you in that tool shed last night. It would have been a disaster if you hadn't been keeping watch. However, we still have another big challenge; we need to get more water from the well. Let's have a meeting again tonight and make some plans."

"We'll be back again tonight, two hours after sunset," promised Extreme Courage.

The whole crew of young radicals was back that night at the tool shed. They were all buzzing with the news about the jungle dwellers. What a miraculous turn of events! They also wanted to see the growth of the potted trees. Once again, they were very excited by what they saw because the trees were at least a foot tall.

"Listen to me, everyone," said Patient Hope. "We want to keep this meeting short. You all need to get as much sleep as possible. As you know, more water will be needed to keep the soil moist in these pots. We believe that we have a better way to get water out of the well. I have just talked with Strong Support and Quiet Meekness, who have been down in the well. The main problem is the ledge about thirty feet down that narrows the opening. It stopped our first bucket and it stopped Strong Support."

"If we use a narrower but longer bucket, then we believe that we should be able to get it past the ledge going down and coming back up with not too much effort. We already found a bucket, which we believe we can modify for that purpose. If we can keep the width of the bucket down to about five inches, then we should be able to get past the ledge."

"We will follow the same procedures that we followed the first time, it should go much quicker, but we do want to bring back as much Living Water as possible. We will not only fill up the narrow bucket, but we will bring several other buckets and fill them from the bucket we dip. The buckets will all then be carried back to our individual homes because the tool shed is getting too crowded to store any more important items. It's hard enough to keep the pots hidden from sight. Fortunately, no one has been working these fields for a couple of weeks, and we have been the only ones using the shed. But you never know when someone might drop in to borrow a tool for another location."

"Extreme Courage will take over from here, and he will be in charge of the whole operation again. I am going back to my house to get some sleep. I didn't sleep well last night, wondering how we were going to keep the trees hidden. Also, Strong Support will invite Devoted Worshipper to watch this operation, since he has been praying for this for so long. That's all from me…good night everyone."

Chapter Ten

THE FRUIT

The strategy appeared to be working. It was obviously being coordinated by the Original Founder, Who was certainly watching over His unusual team of young radicals and a pure-hearted pioneer of the older generation.

The jungle dwellers kept their word, in obedience to their own witch doctor, and cleared a rectangular section of land in the jungle, half way between their own village and the edge of the jungle where the broccoli fields were growing. It was deep enough into the jungle that no one from Veggie Village would see it and very few other jungle dwellers would ever happen to pass that way. Most Normal Jungle dwellers were afraid to get close to Veggie Village because of the stories their ancestors had passed on to them.

MORE LIVING WATER

The middle-of-the-night expedition to the Well of Living Water was also a great success. Just like they had planned, the irregularly-shaped bucket was able to pass through the narrow slot between the rock ledges and several larger containers were filled with Living Water. Those who lived with other young radicals brought the Living Water home to keep it safe until it was needed.

Devoted Worshipper was thrilled to see the open well and the water being drawn from it. He was given his own container of the Living Water and was promised some of the fruit when the trees began to produce.

JOURNEY TO THE JUNGLE

As they had promised, the jungle dwellers came back two days after their first visit. They escorted Patient Hope, Extreme Courage and Strong Support through the jungle paths to the new clearing. They were delighted to see some beautiful jungle birds and the odd animal scurrying away as they followed their new friends.

Soon they arrived at a freshly cut clearing. "This looks perfect," said Patient Hope. "It should be ready to plant the trees tomorrow."

The following morning at sunrise, several of the young radicals were able to excuse themselves from working in the fields, and they helped their leaders carry the three to four-foot potted trees and some of the Living Water into the jungle. The natives watched the planting process with great interest. When they had finally planted all eighteen trees in the ground and watered them with the Living Water, the two men they had met in the broccoli fields approached them and beckoned for them to follow. They were led to a large hut where an older man was sitting in the entrance.

"My chief," declared the man. The chief rose to greet Patient Hope and the others.

"Very nice to meet you," said Patient Hope. "We bring good news. The Great Spirit of our Original Founder will help your people. And because you are helping us plant the miracle fruit, your people will be blessed."

The chief bowed low before Patient Hope and said, "We will hear more about the Original Founder and His Great Spirit. Already some of our children are feeling better. You must come and speak about these in four nights on the full moon. I will gather all the village people and you can speak with them."

"We will come back as you desire," said Patient Hope. "We will tell you the story of the Original Founder. Your people will like this true story very much. Now we must return to our village, if you will excuse us. Again, we thank you for helping us."

Returning to Veggie Village, Patient Hope and the young radicals were buzzing with excitement. Not only did they have the trees planted in a hidden place, but they had the incredible opportunity to share the good news of the Original Founder to the whole village. Was that not what the Original Founder had asked them to do when He departed from Miracle Fruit City?

After two days, Extreme Courage and Faithful Support journeyed back into the jungle to check on their new little orchard. To their surprise, the trees were now six to eight feet in height and most of them already were sporting beautiful, large blossoms.

"Oh my goodness!" exclaimed Strong Support. "Look at those trees! The bees are already cross-pollinating the flowers."

"When we come back in two days on the full moon, we may already have fruit growing," added Extreme Courage. "Wouldn't that be awesome if we could actually give the natives some of the fruit that they helped us grow?"

"That would be so amazing! I pray that will come to pass," said Strong Support.

Returning home, they shared the incredible news with their friends. Everyone was overjoyed and praying for the coming meeting when the story of their Original Founder would be shared with a whole jungle village.

The Big Event

Finally, the anticipated day came. One by one the young radicals slipped away from their homes and their work in the fields. They headed for the jungle, which was a place they had always feared, but now a place that captivated them with extreme excitement. They all wanted to arrive before dark to see the trees in the bright daylight.

Patient Hope and Extreme Courage were the first to arrive. The jungle dwellers were faithfully guarding the trees and were excited to see them. They shouted out at the top of their lungs, "Look at the fruit! Look at the fruit!"

Sure enough, on every tree there were not only blossoms, but there was also an abundance of fruit in every stage of growth. Every tree had some fruit that was fully ripe and ready to eat, each with its unique color, size and shape.

Patient Hope walked from tree to tree in silent awe. Then he began to weep like he had wept when the Original Founder had spoken to him many months before. His dream had come to pass, and his heart was overflowing with passionate love for the Original Founder. How could he ever thank Him enough for allowing him to be the one village elder so deeply involved in the restoration of the original miracle fruit?

Once again, Patient Hope felt the powerful presence of the Original Founder with him. He clearly heard His voice in the depth of his heart. "I want you to share the first-fruits with the jungle village. Tell them the story and then let them taste the fruit with you. I will do special miracles as you share this fruit with them."

"I am Your servant, Original Founder. I will do anything you ask of me," replied the weeping village elder.

One by one the young radicals arrived at the miracle fruit orchard, and they were all in awe of the sight of fresh fruit growing on trees that had been little green shoots just a few days before. Each one of them dropped to their knees and gave thanks to the Original Founder. What would this mean for the future of their village and Normal Jungle? In view of this miracle, it seemed like nothing they could imagine would be impossible in the future.

At Patient Hope's request, a large hand-woven basket was brought to the orchard. Extreme Courage and Strong Support had the privilege of picking the first fruit from each of the eighteen trees. The big basket was full and over-flowing by the time they picked all the ripe fruit.

When they finished the joyful task, they brought the basket to the center of the village. When everyone had been quieted down, the village chief addressed the villagers and asked them to honor and respect their special guests. Then he pointed to Patient Hope and asked him to please speak to the people.

Patient Hope shared from his heart the whole story of the coming of the Original Founder to the ancient jungle. He told them how He had been murdered by jealous men, but the Great Spirit had raised Him from the dead. Then he told them how the Original Founder had given them the miracle fruit and a special Well of Living Water to water the trees.

He shared how the Well of Living Water was in the center of the main street in Miracle Fruit City, and how it had originally been full to the brim and often bubbling over. People loved to drink from the well and shared the water with those who would drink of it wherever they went.

Those who ate this fruit could do amazing things to help other people. He shared how a beautiful city was established with the name of Miracle Fruit City.

Patient Hope went on to tell them that the Original Founder had also commanded them to share the fruit with people who lived in the jungle. The original followers had obeyed His commands and Miracle Fruit City had grown deep into the jungle, and many jungle dwellers had become a part of this wonderful city.

Patient Hope also informed the eager listeners that not everyone was happy with these events. Some leaders opposed the spread of this city into the jungle and persecuted the followers of the Original Founder. Even though they were persecuted, the city continued to grow, and many more jungle dwellers became a part of the city, and the miracle fruit trees were planted in many parts of the jungle as an extension of Miracle Fruit City.

Finally, the persecution had greatly lessened and life became easier for the followers of the Original Founder. However, they soon got busy with other things and their love for the Original Founder grew cold. They forgot to lovingly care for the fruit trees and some of the trees died.

At the same time, the water level in the well was going down lower and lower. After some time had passed, the well was finally covered up because no one wanted to bother with this well when there were many other wells that were easier to draw from. Without the Living Water, the fruit trees no longer produced much fruit and it had lost its miracle power. Eventually, the elders voted to chop the fruit trees down, and they planted more vegetables in their place.

Patient Hope then shared the story of Fearless Dreamer and how he had been visited by the Original Founder and given instructions to save the seeds. Finally, he shared his own story about being a young radical and being told to wait until the proper time for the fruit to be restored.

As Patient Hope shared these facts, the natives were totally engrossed with his story and became very emotionally involved. You could see the sadness on their faces when they heard that the people had allowed the fruit trees to be cut down and the Living Water to be covered up. However, you could also see the excitement in their countenances when he shared about their adventures recovering the hidden treasure.

"And now," Patient Hope concluded, "The Spirit of the Original Founder spoke to me that we must share the first fruits of the miracle fruit with you because you have helped us grow this wonderful fruit. We will cut the fruit into small pieces and pass them out so everyone can taste this wonderful gift from our Original Founder."

The basket of fruit and a small makeshift table were brought out to them. Several of the young radicals began to cut the fruit into bite-sized samples, and the villagers lined up to receive their portion. At the center of every kind of fruit were seeds just like the ones they had planted. Every seed was carefully saved and placed in another container.

Tasting the Fruit

The chief was given a generous portion first, and everyone watched as he placed the juicy morsel into his mouth. The expression on his face was a combination of delight and surprise. He had never tasted anything like it. Not only was it the sweetest food he had ever tasted, but it seemed like it was alive in his mouth because of the tingling feeling it gave him.

Each one of the villagers expressed the same delight and surprise as they tasted the various fruit from the miracle fruit trees. One man sitting in the dirt did not come forward for some reason. Quiet Meekness noticed him and took him a piece of fruit. She put the fruit in the man's mouth and then watched as he began to move his legs and start weeping. He finally reached out his hand and allowed Quiet Meekness to help him up. He then began to walk and jump excitedly. She had no idea that he had been totally paralyzed below the waist. Everyone began pointing at him and shouting out loud.

Another man cried out. "I can hear again, I can hear again!" Once again the crowd shouted excitedly.

Encourage, the young radicals continued to pass out the fruit. After all the natives had partaken of the fruit, several more exciting miracles spontaneously occurred. The excitement among the crowd was electric.

Next, the young radicals turned to Patient Hope and insisted that he taste the fruit before them. He had been waiting for this day much longer than they had and he deserved it.

Patient Hope bowed his head and gave thanks out loud for all to hear. It was a moment none of them would ever forget. He tried to keep his composure in front of the villagers, but just three words into his prayer of thanksgiving, he broke down emotionally. When he finally finished his prayer, he put a piece of fruit into his mouth.

The fruit released sensations in his mouth that he had never felt before. It was like a fire-cracker was going off in his mouth, but without any pain – only pleasure. He closed his eyes and savored it for as long as he could before swallowing it. Then he looked up at the crowd and thanked them for the wonderful privilege of serving them the beautiful fruit, provided by the Original Founder of Miracle Fruit City. He then left them with a challenge. He asked them to decide whether they would forsake all other gods that they had previously worshipped and believe in the Original Founder, or keep their other gods instead. He promised to return in two days to find out their decision.

As soon as Patient Hope finished speaking, the crowd became very noisy as the people talked with each other about this new idea. They all said good-bye and the young radicals and Patient Hope headed home, happier than they had ever been in their entire lives.

On their way back through the jungle and the broccoli fields, some of the young radicals experienced an abundance of overwhelming joy and broke into laughing and back-slapping, while others felt more love and compassion than they had ever imagined possible. They longed passionately to return to the jungle village and bless the natives. Still others felt an amazing, powerful peace overwhelm their spirits, chasing away every bit of fear and worry, even though they knew that some real problems could arise as a result of their adventures with the fruit.

They were all feeling something special deep down in their souls, and they knew instinctively that it had something to do with the miracle fruit they had eaten that night. When they finally got back to their homes, they slept a deep and peaceful sleep. However, a number of them had unusual dreams that gave them knowledge of things to come in the village and in the jungle. The next day they compared notes and found many similarities in their dreams.

Chapter Eleven

THE CONFRONTATION

Early the next morning, Patient Hope heard a loud knock on his front door. He arose from his chair and went to investigate who would be calling on him at this early hour. It was probably one of the young radicals who couldn't wait to tell him something new.

Instead, he opened the door to look into the faces of two very serious-looking village elders. The older man, named Narrow Minded, was a tall man with a no-nonsense reputation, and Patient Hope knew him well. He was from his own district and this was the elder that he was the most concerned about. The younger man, Timid Follower, was rather short and stocky. A bit surprised, Patient Hope paused as he looked into their faces, and then he quickly greeted them, "Good morning brothers, please come in and have a seat."

The two men sat down in the squeaky old chairs that Patient Hope had pulled out for them, and Narrow Minded cleared his throat self-consciously and proceeded to address his host, "Patient Hope, we have been hearing rumors about you and I fear they are true."

"We have been watching your behavior and where you have been spending your time. You have been seen several times with Extreme Courage, Faithful Support and several other young radicals who have been carrying on with this crazy dream of restoring the miracle fruit trees to Veggie Village. They have not submitted to our leadership for some time, and we believe that you are encouraging their rebellion."

"Patient Hope, you are highly respected by most of the residents of Veggie Village. You must change your behavior or face the discipline of our district elders. Your punishment, as you know, would include being stripped of your status as village elder. It might also include public flogging and imprisonment. If that doesn't change your mind, then you know that there are even more serious punishments for those who refuse to submit to the traditions of the elders."

"On the other hand, you could just renounce your association with the young radicals, making a statement of your disbelief in the restoration of the ancient fruit or the possibility that seeds are still hidden that could be planted today. We would prefer that option."

Patient Hope once again sensed that in spite of the words of this hard-hearted elder, he was feeling the almost tangible presence of the Original Founder and a Spirit of Wisdom coming over him.

He paused for a moment and then slowly responded, "Yes, my dear friend, I am aware of the justice system of Veggie Village, and I thank you for coming to inform me of your suspicions and express your concerns. I do not wish to make a statement at this time as to whether I support or denounce the restoration theory, but I can assure you that I have a clear conscience regarding my association with the young radicals."

"I also believe very strongly that the purpose for which I was born was to bring wisdom and guidance to these idealistic young men and women, and I do believe I am doing just that. In fact, I believe that many of the elders and residents of Veggie Village will be very happy with the fruit of my association with them."

Patient Hope could not help but smile as he spoke that last statement and realized the unintended play on words. He knew deep inside that the miracle fruit would indeed bring great happiness to many folk in Veggie Village, even though some of the elders were most likely to be very angry about it. He was confident in the depths of his heart that the power of the fruit would convince everyone who was open minded of its value, unlike his guest.

"Well," retorted the still-frowning elder, "we'll see about that."

"I'll tell you what," said Patient Hope, his heart surging with fresh wisdom from the Original Founder, "Let's have a meeting in three days in the open square at the heart of our district. We'll invite everyone in the district, including all the elders, to come, and you and any witnesses can state your case against me. Let me then speak in my own defense and present my witnesses, according to the long-held tradition of our village. Every accused person has the right to present his defense before the people and the elders."

"Well if that's what you want, then that's what you shall get. Just remember that once you've had your chance to speak, your punishment can come swiftly."

"Yes, Narrow Minded, I am certainly aware of those consequences. As I said, I believe the fruit of my relationship with the young radicals will make many people happy in Veggie Village."

"Then we will see you in three days at the open square at high noon."

"I will certainly be there, Narrow Minded. It was nice to see you too, Timid Follower. Come again some time."

The two elders left the house with their frowns intact on their unhappy faces. Patient Hope knew that his work was cut out for him, and he would have to be more careful about who was watching him. He needed to connect with Extreme Courage and put together a strategy for the open-square gathering because he only had one chance to get it right. He breathed a prayer of thanksgiving and another prayer of petition for more wisdom and guidance. He was not afraid because he was confident that the Original Founder would not desert him now.

Patient Hope did briefly connect with Extreme Courage, although he knew he was probably being watched. They quickly agreed upon a strategy, and they made plans to return to the jungle village the following day. They wanted to see what was happening with the trees and what decision the village people had made.

THE BIG DECISION

To avoid unnecessary attention, just the two of them journeyed into the jungle to visit the village just beyond their new orchard. As they passed the orchard, they noticed the trees had grown even larger, and there was an abundance of beautiful, luscious-looking fruit.

When they arrived at the edge of the village, they were greeted with great excitement. From the younger children to the elderly, they were chattering loudly at once, each trying to be heard above the others. It was hard to understand anything with everyone talking at once, but they could clearly tell that more miracles had definitely taken place.

Escorted into the center of the village by the excited crowd, they found themselves standing in front of the village chief and the resident witch doctor, who had been absent at their previous meeting. The chief motioned the crowd to be quiet so that he could speak.

"Patient Hope and Extreme Courage," he began slowly and deliberately, "we have been talking much with all of our people, including our spiritual leader. He now agrees with us that your Original Founder is the One our village should worship, and not the gods we have served in the past. They have no power that can compare to the power of the Great Spirit of the Original Founder."

"We have seen many miracles take place since we ate some of the fruit from the trees. Two blind men are now seeing, three cripples are walking and another old deaf lady is hearing again. Our babies are all well and there is great joy instead of sadness. We wish to be taught how to know your Original Founder. We want to eat your fruit and also your vegetables. We will change our village according to your instructions. We will do all that we can to please the Original Founder of your village."

Patient Hope tried to keep his composure while his heart wanted to weep with gratitude for what he was hearing. After a short pause, he replied, "I am very happy to hear about your decision. We will be pleased to teach you what we know about the Original Founder and the best ways to worship and serve Him. We will return to your village soon and begin to teach you His ways, but first I need to ask you something else."

Patient Hope and Extreme Courage then shared their situation and their strategy with the chief. He was very eager to help, and soon they said their good-byes and prepared to depart.

Before leaving, they encouraged the people to eat the fruit as it ripened and to always save the seeds, so that more trees could be planted. On the way home, the two happy radicals filled the baskets they had brought with fruit, so they could share another portion with the other radicals.

Patient Hope on Trial

By mid-afternoon the public square in the middle of their district began to fill up with curious villagers and elders. Patient Hope arrived early and took his place at the front with the other elders. As he looked to his left and right and then out into the crowd, he realized that Narrow Minded had not only invited the elders and people from their own district, but from all the other districts of Veggie Village. At this point, Patient Hope realized how high the stakes had been raised. Narrow Minded was lining up his heavy artillery against him, hoping to kill the fruit restoration movement once and for all.

Among the other stern-faced elders, Patient Hope noticed Rule Keeper, his new ally from the south end of the village. Their eyes met momentarily and Rule Keeper flashed Patient Hope a quick smile and a wink, which assured him that he had not changed his mind since their special time of examining the ancient scrolls together.

The atmosphere in the front was rather tense, as elders greeted one another with plastic smiles and handshakes. The people back in the crowd were more curious than concerned, and it was a time for them to say hi to old friends as they waited for the leaders to start the meeting.

Narrow Minded finally stepped up to the antique pulpit reserved for the larger village gatherings. Raising his voice to be heard above the conversation, he called for order and quiet.

"Citizens of Veggie Village, kindly give me your attention please. I want you to know that we have a very serious situation in our sacred village. We want to honor our Original Founder and keep our village pure and free of those who would disgrace it by not honoring our long-held traditions, which have been passed on to us by our holy ancestors."

"We are calling this special assembly today to inform you that not only do we have the normal wild-eyed young people challenging the authority and spirituality of the village elders, but one of the long-respected elders has been taking sides with them. He has actually encouraged and facilitated their rebellion in certain matters."

"The elder in question is Patient Hope, and we are going to convince you that he must be disciplined severely, unless he publicly denounces his partnership with this rebellious generation. He will be given the opportunity to speak for himself, which will either seal his punishment with his rebellious attitude, or he can recant and renounce this foolishness by asking all of us for forgiveness."

"Please listen carefully now, as we present the evidence against Patient Hope. I would like to ask Suspicious Observer to please come forward and tell us what he has witnessed with his own eyes."

"My dear friends and loyal citizens of Veggie Village," Suspicious Observer began. "As you know, I have very keen eyesight, even in the dark. Because of this special gift, I don't always retire when others do to save their candles after dark. I like to go for walks in the cool night air. Over the last few weeks, I have observed a number of young men and women heading in the same direction at different intervals towards the tool shed in the nearby broccoli field at the edge of Normal Jungle."

"This happened several times in the last few weeks. I thought it was rather strange, so I decided to pay closer attention. Then I noticed that the older one was actually one of the village elders, and I easily recognized him by the way he walked. Then I saw him meet up with Extreme Courage, and they went into the tool shed together. I know that Extreme Courage has been a leader of those who would like to change our traditions, so I immediately told Narrow Minded about it, as any good citizen would do."

"Thank you Suspicious Observer," said Narrow Minded. "Now I'd like to call Elder Timid Follower to come and share what he has witnessed."

Timid Follower began nervously, "Well, uh, I just want to say, uh, that is, I was asked by, uh, Narrow Minded to go and investigate, uh, you know, what was happening over there at the tool shed. So, uh, I went out there, uh, about oh, about two days ago. Yes, it was two days ago, as I recall. Well, uh, when I went to the uh, broccoli field there, I saw a strange thing. Uh, there were a lot of places in the field that had been destroyed. The, uh, crop was, you know, badly damaged in those places. I can't really imagine what those, uh, young whipper-snappers were doing that would destroy the broccoli crop just before the, uh, harvest. But, uh, obviously, they're up to no good in my humble opinion."

"And what about the tool shed?" interrupted Narrow Minded impatiently. "What did you find in the tool shed?"

"Uh, well, it seemed to me that they had been using those tools in there. And, uh, I found an odd shaped bucket in the corner with some water in it. I found some rope that, uh, had never been there before. I think the radicals had been, uh, messing around with stuff in there and, like I said, you know, they are not up to any good."

"Thank you, Timid Follower," Narrow Minded said. "As you can all see, these stubborn and rebellious young people have obviously damaged the broccoli crop. What have they been up to in that tool shed and elsewhere? It seems that when the good, law-abiding citizens are peacefully resting in their beds, these wild-eyed kids are up to their rebellious mischief."

Narrow Minded then accused the young radicals of dishonoring the

Original Founder. How could they possibly imagine that they could regrow the same fruit that He had planted many, many centuries before? What made them think that planting fruit seeds and eating fruit would enable them to do the same things the Original Founder had done?

Then Narrow Minded provided evidence that Patient Hope had also been a young radical as a youth, but he had appeared to have gotten over it. Now it looked like he had reverted to the foolishness of his youth, when he should have been wiser at this late stage in his life.

Narrow Minded concluded, "I'm sure you will all agree with me that any elder who meets with these crazy young radicals and supports their destructive activities should no longer be given the honor of being called a Veggie Village elder. After Patient Hope has had his say, which our village laws require, I am going to ask you to support us as we impose whatever punishment on Patient Hope that we feel he deserves."

"I will now invite Patient Hope to repent of his rebellious ways or to explain why, as a Veggie Village elder, he has betrayed the entire village and its elders. So please, Patient Hope, you may address us now."

All eyes were on Patient Hope as he slowly but confidently approached the antique pulpit. For several seconds, he scanned the audience from left to right. Finally, he opened his mouth and began his defense.

"Respected village elders and all of the hard-working citizens of Veggie Village: I have come to you fully aware that this could be my very last opportunity to speak with all of you. I know that my behavior has been very difficult for the elders and citizens of Veggie Village to understand. So I request that you to pay very close attention to my explanation."

"As I declared to Narrow Minded when he visited me in my home three days ago, 'I believe the village will be very happy with the fruit of my relationship with what have been called the rebellious radicals.' I realize that I have not held to the traditions of our current elders, but I have strived to return to the pure teaching of our Original Founder and the ancient elders who served Him so well."

"I realize that most of our well-educated elders are convinced that what the Original Founder and the original elders experienced cannot and will not ever occur again. However, I have never in my life fully accepted that belief. Somewhere, deep inside my soul, I felt that the Original Founder would want us to restore the fullness of what the ancient elders had enjoyed after His departure from this community."

Narrow Minded was getting visibly angry, wishing he didn't have to allow Patient Hope to speak. He exchanged frowns with the other elders sitting near him and then turned back towards Patient Hope to hear what he would say next.

Patient Hope continued, "It has been correctly reported that when I was young, I was one of the young radicals. I was as convinced as any of them that our village could once again enjoy the blessings of the original miracle fruit. As time went on, many of the other young radicals gave up their pursuit of the fruit. Consequently, I became very frustrated and prayed to the Original Founder that He would tell me what to do."

"I know this may be hard for you to understand, but the Original Founder did answer my prayer. He visited me in a very special way and spoke clearly to my spirit. He told me to have patience and keep my hope that the fruit would be restored, but to be quiet about it until the right time came. I have been waiting these many decades."

Narrow Minded could no longer restrain himself, "And you'll still be waiting when they put you in the grave. There will never be any fruit in Veggie Village again."

"Well, Narrow Minded, I'm so sorry to upset you, but I must go on. My waiting has not been in vain. No indeed, it has not been in vain. It's a very long story, which I would be happy to tell in a future meeting, but we have already proven you wrong. Listen to me honored elders and citizens of Veggie Village. The Founding Father spoke to me once again, and He told me that now was the time. These young radicals would help me, or rather I would help them, find the seeds, which would then be planted and once more the miracle fruit would be grown. I want to announce to you that we have already found the seeds. We have grown and eaten the precious fruit, and we have experienced its amazing power."

"We have also discovered the original Well of Living Water that was used to water the fruit trees. It has allowed us to grow this wonderful fruit in a hurry. And one more thing – this village was not originally called Veggie Village – it was called, 'Miracle Fruit City'. Our beloved Original Founder never intended us to live on veggies alone, but on a balanced diet, which included a generous portion of this wonderful fruit. We were known far and wide not for our vegetables, but for our fruit."

Narrow Minded was now beside himself with rage, but for a moment he was speechless. Patient Hope took advantage of that moment and quickly spoke up again.

"Honored Elders and citizens, wouldn't you like to see the results of this amazing discovery?"

Everyone looked at one another and then at the elders, but they were a little fearful to speak out.

Patient Hope quickly followed with a question that demanded an answer, "Would you like to see the sick healed, the blind see and the lame walk? Don't be afraid. Speak the truth without fear, like our Original Founder did."

A young crippled lady was the first to respond, "Yes, I would!"

An old blind man shouted out, "Me too!"

Then young and old cried out in waves of, "Yes! Yes! Yes! Fruit! Fruit! Fruit!"

With that, Patient Hope turned to his right and waved to Extreme Courage, who was waiting in the wings. Extreme Courage waived to a number of others, and they worked their way towards Patient Hope and the antique pulpit.

As they approached, Patient Hope signaled the crowd to quiet down, so he could speak to them again.

THE CONFRONTATION

"Look at this," he shouted. "Here are six young radicals, whom I have been working with, and here are six new friends from Normal Jungle who have decided, along with their entire village, to become part of the new Miracle Fruit City. They have been helping us grow the fruit in a clearing in the jungle. If we can grow fruit in various parts of the city and then expand into the jungle, which they are also willing to clear, we can see this city grow again like it did at the beginning."

Patient Hope then addressed the twelve people he had invited to the platform. "Now please take the coverings off your baskets and show the people what you have there."

All twelve removed the cloth coverings from their baskets. There, before their bulging eyes was the largest, most beautiful, and luscious-looking fruit that anyone had ever seen. Of course, most of the Veggie Village residents had never seen fruit before, so they were truly in awe.

Narrow Minded had already seen too much. "You have no right to bring that fruit up here," he blurted out.

"But you know that I have a right to bring witnesses and evidence for the people to see and judge for themselves, so we will continue," responded Patient Hope.

"And now, I'd like to present to you the chief of the nearest village, which is located not too far into Normal Jungle and close to our district's broccoli fields. Please listen to what he has to say."

The chief began a little cautiously, but he quickly gained confidence. "Greetings, citizens and elders of Veggie Village: I am a new believer in your Original Founder, whom you all worship. A few weeks ago, our village was under a very terrible plague. Our babies and young children were getting very sick and they were dying very quickly. Our witch doctor told us that the Veggie Village people had put a curse on us and that we should attack them."

"So we decided to send six strong young warriors into Veggie Village during the night to destroy your crops. We planned on starting in the broccoli fields and then moving field to field, destroying as much as we could before daylight. The young warriors just got started in your broccoli fields when they heard a terrible noise and felt like they were going to be attacked. They ran home and talked to the witch doctor. He told them that your gods must be stronger than ours, and we must come and ask for your forgiveness and seek your help."

"We sent two of our men to talk with your people and met Patient Hope and Extreme Courage. They asked us to clear land for the fruit trees and we agreed. The trees and fruit grew very fast, like magic. Even before we ate the fruit, our children started to feel better. Then they brought us the fruit and told us we could also become believers in your Original Founder, Who gave you the fruit."

"After all of us agreed to serve Him, including our witch doctor, many other exciting things began to happen. This young lady was crippled from birth and now you see her walking. These two old men were blind and now they have perfect vision. This lady was deaf and now she hears like the rest of us. Not one of our babies has gotten sick, and we believe your Original Founder has accepted us as His followers."

"But the most exciting thing is that we have felt peace and joy in our hearts and love for one another. We even have a wonderful love for you in Veggie Village. We always thought you were very strange and even dangerous, and we kept our children from ever going near Veggie Village."

"We would now actually like to become a part of your new Miracle Fruit City. We will cut down more of the jungle and grow more trees between our village and yours, but we will need more Living Water from your well, so the seeds can produce the miracle trees with the miracle fruit."

Patient Hope stepped back up to the pulpit and shouted, "Do you citizens of Veggie Village also want the Living Water from the ancient well and the miracle fruit from the ancient seeds? Do you want to become part of Miracle Fruit City?"

THE CONFRONTATION

"YES! YES! YES!" came the overwhelming and almost deafening response.

Just then another tall and lean figure approached the pulpit and beckoned for the crowd to be quiet. It was Rule Keeper.

"Dear elders and citizens of Veggie Village. As you know, I have been a staunch supporter of our traditions and rules in this village. I have been adamantly opposed to the idea that the fruit could ever be restored. I have persecuted any young radicals in my district, and they have had to change their thinking or leave my district. Until a couple of weeks ago that is, when I had a strange dream. In the dream, I saw fruit trees growing up quickly and spreading throughout the village, which started here in the north and spread to my district in the south. I was told in the dream to cooperate with Patient Hope and become a part of this adventure."

"The next day, Patient Hope came to me and asked to see the ancient scrolls that I have had hidden in my house. We spent more than two days reading these scrolls, and we learned more about the history of our village. We discovered many things, including the original name of Veggie Village, which was Miracle Fruit City, but also about the Well of Living Water."

"I want it put in the record that I am one who will stand by Patient Hope and his younger truth-seekers. I would say that their search has been rewarded. At any rate, if you wish to punish Patient Hope, then you will have to punish me also."

"I can arrange that for sure," Narrow Minded shouted out angrily.

But by now, no one was listening to Narrow Minded. The people began to press in to get a closer look at the incredible fruit.

Patient Hope shouted out again, "We just happen to have a few sharp knives to cut up the fruit so that everyone can have a little taste. We still have some of the original seeds that we found in the Well of Living Water, and soon there will be plenty of fruit for everyone."

"In fact, I know you would all like to see the wonderful fruit trees growing just inside the edge of the jungle. Tomorrow, everyone is welcome to follow us there to see the beautiful trees, and then you can decide if you would like to have them in your neighborhood growing alongside your precious vegetables. Is anyone interested?"

Again the response was an overwhelming, "YES! YES! YES!"

"Then meet us at the old tool shed by the broccoli field tomorrow at noon. We will lead you there and we can join our Normal Jungle friends in the dedication of this orchard to the honor and glory of our wonderful Original Founder."

Then an older gentleman stepped up to the pulpit and said, "My name is Devoted Worshipper. I am not an elder because the elders did not trust me to follow their traditions. However, I have been a worshipper of the Original Founder for my entire life, and I always believed that He would restore the original fruit. One day He showed me where the Well of Living Water was located, and I've been praying over that spot every morning before daybreak for many years. Today, I see the fruit of my prayers, and I am here to stand with Patient Hope and Rule Keeper. I want the same punishment that they get."

Narrow Minded quickly gathered as many of the elders as he could for a mini-conference, but very few wanted to join him. Most of them wanted to taste the fruit. He saw that he couldn't accomplish much that day, so he told the elders to meet with him early the next morning.

In the meantime, everyone else was getting a small taste of the precious fruit, and they were experiencing the same phenomena that the others had earlier. Their countenances began to shine with joy as they experienced the tingling in their mouths and their eyes began to sparkle with excitement. People began to hug one another and cry together with joy over the fact that they had been visited by the Original Founder.

One after another the people turned to Patient Hope and the young radicals to say a heart-felt, "Thank you so much for giving us this wonderful fruit!"

One of the younger elders said, "We will never be the same again. We feel so much joy, peace and love. Don't worry, you won't be punished. You deserve a reward for your courage and faithfulness to the Original Founder."

The people suddenly began to grab hands and jump up and down in a spontaneous dance together. None of them had ever danced before in Veggie Village, so it was a very interesting sight to behold. No one really cared what they looked like because they were having too much fun.

Patient Hope observed the wild and chaotically happy scene and began to weep again. Once again it was like he could feel the Original Founder standing at his side just a little bit behind him, looking over his right shoulder. That special presence was the best feeling of all, and nothing could ever compare with that – not even eating the precious fruit. IT WAS HIM! The Original Founder – the One Who had given His very life for him. Patient Hope was thankful that he had been obedient and patient! The joy that he was witnessing and the strong presence of the Original Founder was reward enough, and so much more, for any problems he had ever encountered because of his faith and trust in the Original Founder.

The party eventually came to an end and everyone went home very happy – well, almost everyone.

Chapter Twelve
THE FRUIT OF THE FRUIT

The results of that great meeting were more than could be counted. The original name of Miracle Fruit City was restored, and the jungle was being transformed into a fruitful orchard, with vegetable gardens mixed in for variety. Many jungle dwellers were converted and moved into the ever-growing Miracle Fruit City.

The rest of the original seeds were planted in three districts of Miracle Fruit City. They responded to the Living Water just like the others had. The residents kept every seed from their fruit, so they could plant trees in other places, and soon fruit trees were growing up all over the city.

Another miracle also took place. Do you remember the Well of Living Water and how difficult it was for the young radicals to get to the water at the beginning? Well, the water level rose dramatically after the people ate the fruit and embraced the new life-style. In fact, the water came right to the top of the well, like it had been at the beginning. Furthermore, there appeared to be a fountain within the well that came bubbling up to the top. The water was always moving and never stagnant, and at times it overflowed onto the city square.

The residents decided to make channels for the overflow and dug paths for the Living Water. When the water bubbled over, it flowed into the communities and watered their fruit trees and vegetables, which resulted in great increase and prosperity throughout Miracle Fruit City.

Some of the young radicals had wondered why the water level had been so low when they rediscovered the well, but it had obviously been that low when the seeds had been hidden on the lower ledge. Patient Hope asked the Original Founder about this and was informed that the level of unbelief in the community had caused the water to subside and stay at a very low level.

Drawing water from the well had become very difficult and the leaders finally decided to just cover it up. However, Fearless Dreamer had been able to place the seed container on the lower ledge before the well was covered up, knowing that someone would find the seeds when they were looking for the Living Water.

When the faith level rose in the community, the water level rose in the well, and it became much easier to access, drink or pour on the ground where the seeds were planted.

There was only one sad thing to report. Narrow Minded was able to keep a small number of elders and residents under his influence, and they became very bitter and even more narrow-minded than before. They chose to come together in the south end of Miracle Fruit City and separate themselves from the fruit-loving residents. They built a high wall around their neighborhood, which would keep out everyone who believed in the power of the fruit. They put up signs that read: "Veggie Village – No Fruit Lovers Welcome".

The rest of Miracle Fruit City, however, loved their fruit and they shared it with everyone they could. More and more of the young radicals, whose ranks had multiplied many times, decided to go into the vast darkness of the jungle to share the good news with those living in hopelessness and despair.

They all carried seeds from their fruit, as well as from their vegetables. They also carried a vessel with Living Water from their well to water the seeds whenever people received the message of the love of their Original Founder, who had sacrificed Himself for them. The people would clear space in their jungle home for the fruit trees. Then the young radicals would water the seeds with the Living Water, and the fruit trees and the vegetables would grow like nothing the people had ever seen.

They would also dig fresh wells and pour a few drops of the Living Water into the new well. The life in those few drops of Living Water transformed the whole well into another Well of Living Water.

Not everyone believed the young radicals, but their beautiful countenances and the amazing stories they shared were enough to convince many Normal Jungle residents, and frequently whole communities, to embrace the strange but wonderful good news. It wasn't long before the jungle was changing dramatically. Every area of the jungle was affected because there was far less darkness and much more light. The fame of Miracle Fruit City spread far and wide throughout the whole jungle.

Even where the community leaders resisted the good news, there would be people who became believers, and they gathered together and cleared space in their region to plant fruit trees and vegetables. As they cleared and planted, the jungle gave way to more light. The power of the darkness was being broken, fewer crimes were committed, there was less death and violence and more respect was shown for others.

This story is just about over, and it would be nice to say that everyone lived happily ever after, but that would be a bit of an exaggeration. The elders and residents of Veggie Village became more aggressive and persecuted those who accepted the good news brought by Patient Hope and the young radicals. They found others who were angry or bitter for some reason and got them to join forces with them to attack the hated "Fruit Lovers" as often as possible.

There were also some very wicked people in the heart of the jungle who hated the bearers of good news as well. They were influenced by a very different spirit than the Spirit of the Original Founder of Miracle Fruit City. The more the jungle was changing for good, the angrier these people became. Their numbers had declined significantly, but their fury had only increased.

Thus, the battle continues to rage. However, the servants of the

Original Founder are full of confidence that whatever happens, His presence will always be with them. As long as they continue to partake of the miracle fruit and the Living Water, they will be filled with peace, joy and love.

They have also read enough of the ancient and most sacred scrolls to glean what the Original Founder had promised in clear language that He will return once again in all His great glory, and as the Chief Elder, He will dwell in Miracle Fruit City and His kindness will never depart from it.

They also reported that those who continue to resist His servants will be punished according to their crimes, but to those who have been faithful and loyal, He will bring incredible rewards with great honor and glory.

Miracle Fruit City dwellers are really looking forward to that exciting day.

P.S. You may have wished for a little romance woven into the story, but you may have guessed that Strong Support and Quiet Meekness were attracted to each other. Yes, they were eventually married. Our other young hero, Extreme Courage hit it off with Gentle Compassion, who was a great blessing to him. Both couples raised a beautiful, fruitful crop of young radicals who continued the work of their radical and fruitful parents.

Addendum

The Veggie Village story is an allegory, but not every detail can be taken as symbolic of a particular church condition, etc.

At the same time, there are many symbolic situations and events in the story with which the reader might appreciate a little help in understanding.

The book was written without a clear plot in mind and I believe much of it came by inspiration. After it was written, some of the hidden meaning was revealed to me. I will try to explain some of those things, as well as some of the obvious ones.

Symbolism in "Veggie Village and the Great and Dangerous Jungle"

1. The seeds are the Living Word of God, both the written Word and the anointed spoken or prophetic Word. God said He would put His words in our mouth and the mouths of our children. (Isaiah 59:21) Peter commanded us to speak "as the oracles of God". (I Peter 4:11)
2. The Living Water is the Holy Spirit. Without the Holy Spirit the Word has no power. The Spirit empowers the Word, just like

the Living Water empowers the seed to produce living fruit.
3. The Fruit and Gifts are intertwined and interdependent. This is how it works:

Faith is the key to all of the gifts of the Holy Spirit. Without faith it is impossible to please God. All gifts require faith to operate.

The Bible says that faith works by love. (Galatians 5:6)

Love is the key to all the fruit. All the spiritual fruit depends on love, and without love, the gifts have no benefit for us who serve them. (I Corinthians 13)

When we have true Holy Spirit empowered love, faith comes. When faith comes, the other spiritual gifts can be activated. Joy and peace, and all the other fruit, also create an atmosphere for faith and miracles.

Some people argue that we don't need the gifts; we just need the fruit, which is a very unscriptural argument. We absolutely need both. My experience has been that true love, joy and peace are the strongest when the gifts are also functioning. I have witnessed pastors, who had not been talking to each other, come together and repent for their pride when the miracles and revival began to break out. God brought peace, joy and especially love, when the gifts began to operate.

It all started with an amazing missionary, named Jack Schissler, who passionately loved God and Argentina, his adopted nation, and an evangelist, named Elmer Burnette, to whom God had given a deep love for people, as well as the anointing for healing and miracles. I was his young travelling companion and prayer partner. He was the father, and I was the young radical being mentored in the supernatural.

When he began to pour out the love and truth of God to the Bible School and a local church, miracles began to happen as people received the love. The joy and peace of God then began to overwhelm the crowd. The next day, the meetings had to be moved to a large auditorium.

The worship was passionate, like nothing I had never witnessed in North America. The more the loving worship was poured out to God, the more the miracles happened, and the more the miracles happened, the more love was expressed to God and fellow worshippers. The result was a thousand or more souls saved in six weeks, thousands more received the baptism of the Holy Spirit, hundreds of amazing miracles occurred and five new fast-growing churches sprang up in the following year.

4. There were nine different trees, representing the nine spiritual fruit in Galatians 5:22-23, and nine spiritual gifts, recorded in I Corinthians 12:8-10.
5. There were five of each kind of seed. Five is the number of grace, which is released through humility. (James 4:6) The Greek New Testament word for grace is "Charis", while the word for gift is "Charisma", a "thing of grace". God's grace is necessary for the reception and release of spiritual gifts, as well as spiritual fruit.
6. Some of the Normal Jungle dwellers had artificial light. This represents false wisdom - knowledge without divine revelation.
7. Running from the light. Those whose deeds are evil love the darkness and won't come to the light, lest their deeds be exposed. The light of the sun was blinding to them. The Son of God in His glory is frightening to the human soul without intimacy with God.
8. The fruit trees represent believers who have been planted as trees of righteousness. They have been baptized in the Holy Spirit, and they are full of fruit and the power that is released by the fruit. We grow when the Word of God is sown into our hearts on good (soft and fertile) soil.
9. Veggies are like the law and commandments, which protect us from many problems if we obey them. They require sacrifice and

effort. To live on veggies alone requires resisting the temptation to enjoy the pleasures of the world.

Veggies are also what religious spirits determine is right and holy. Modern manifestations include wearing only certain clothing, judging people for the length or shortness of their hair, and going to church loyally, even when there is no life flowing out of it. The Pharisees would have loved Veggie Village.

10. The ancient elders obviously represent the original apostles and the early church fathers.
11. Veggie Village elders living in the traditions of their fathers represent those who carry on religious tradition without a relationship with Jesus, the Original Founder of Christianity.
12. The Young Radicals represent the millions of young people around the world who are crying out to God and seeking Him with passion to see His glory released on the earth. They are seeking His presence and His power. They want to see the book of Acts restored in the church of today. I was one of those young radicals at the age of nineteen in Bible School. In a very real sense, this book was written in my heart then, but not on paper until over four decades later.
13. Patient Hope represents the spiritual fathers and mothers in the church who still believe that God wants to restore His glory on the earth and who are willing to give their lives to a younger generation who want God more than anything else in this world. My goal is to be one of these spiritual fathers on the earth.

Since finishing the original draft of this book, another significant revelation has impacted me. It was simply the fact that many generations of young radicals had come and gone, and none of them were ever successful in their quest. However, when one spiritual father became an ally to the young radicals, they were amazingly successful.

It is my firm belief that God is doing something special in this generation, turning the hearts of the fathers to the children, and the children to the fathers (Malachi 4:5,6). The teamwork between spiritual fathers (and mothers) and young radicals is going to generate incredible revival fires, characterized by the fruit and gifts of the Holy Spirit in unprecedented quantity and quality.

Conclusion

As far as I'm concerned, there are only two positions available in the body of Christ, when it comes to bringing in the great and final Kingdom Harvest:

1. Young Radicals, who are passionate lovers and worshippers of Jesus, doing the work of God with passion, in the power of the Holy Spirit, manifesting the fruit and the gifts of the Holy Spirit.
2. Spiritual Fathers and Mothers, who have gained much wisdom and experience, and who have the same passion for the presence and power of God. They are needed to guide the idealism of youth into the fruitful paths of God.

Which position can you fill? Or perhaps you are one of those who will fill both at the same time.

Ben R. Peters

With over 40 years of ministry experience, Ben Peters with his wife, Brenda, have been called to an international apostolic ministry of equipping and activating others with a passion for sending laborers into the harvest fields of the earth, including the seven mountains of society. As founders and directors first of Open Heart Ministries, and now the Kingdom Sending Center, Ben and Brenda have ministered to tens of thousands with teaching and prophetic ministry. The result is that many have been saved, healed, delivered and activated into powerful ministries of their own.

Ben has been given significant insights for the body of Christ and has written sixteen books in the past ten years, since beginning a full-time itinerant ministry. His passions and insights include unity in the body of Christ, accessing the glory of God, five-fold team ministry, prophetic ministry, and signs and wonders for the world-wide harvest.

Kingdom Sending Center
P.O. Box 25
Genoa, IL 60135

www.KingdomSendingCenter.org
ben.peters@kingdomsendingcenter.org

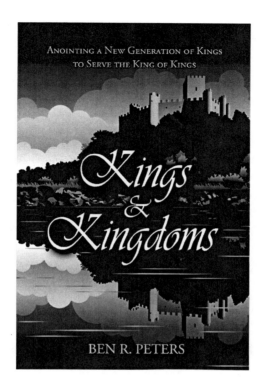

Kings and Kingdoms
Anointing a New Generation of Kings
to Serve the King of Kings
by Ben R. Peters

Available from Kingdom Sending Center
www.kingdomsendingcenter.org

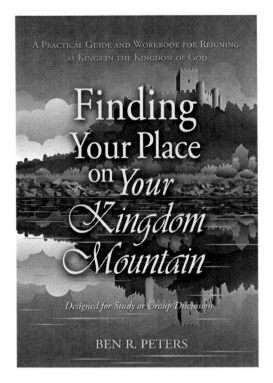

**Finding Your Place
on Your Kingdom Mountain**
A Practical Guide and Workbook for Reigning
as Kings in the Kingdom of God
by Ben R. Peters

Designed for Study or Group Discussion

Available from Kingdom Sending Center
www.kingdomsendingcenter.org

Catching up to the Third World
Seven Indispensable Keys
To EXPLOSIVE Revival
in the Western Church
by Ben R. Peters

Available from Kingdom Sending Center
www.kingdomsendingcenter.org

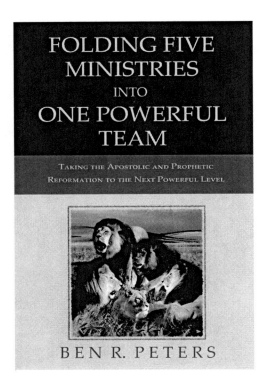

Folding Five Ministries Into One Powerful Team
Taking the Apostolic and Prophetic Reformation
to the Next Powerful Level
by Ben R. Peters

Available from Kingdom Sending Center
www.kingdomsendingcenter.org

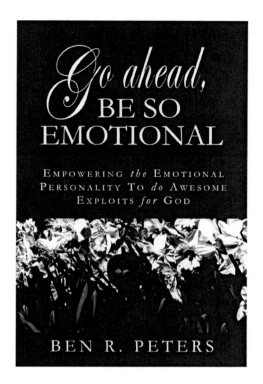

Go Ahead, Be So Emotional
Empowering the Emotional Personality
to do Awesome Exploits for God
by Ben R. Peters

Available from Kingdom Sending Center
www.kingdomsendingcenter.org

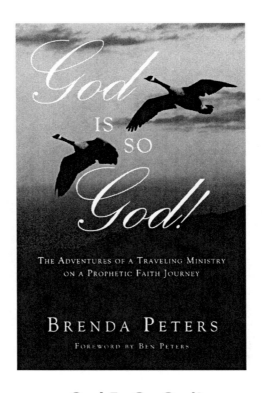

God Is So God!
The Adventures of a Traveling Ministry
on a Prophetic Faith Journey
by Brenda Peters

Available from Kingdom Sending Center
www.kingdomsendingcenter.org

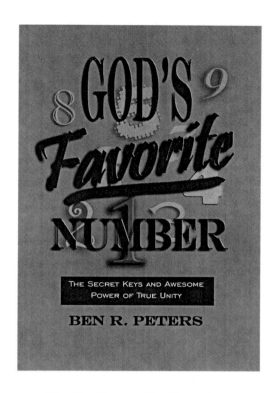

God's Favorite Number
The Secret Keys and Awesome
Power of True Unity
by Ben R. Peters

Available from Kingdom Sending Center
www.kingdomsendingcenter.org

Prophetic Ministry
Strategic Key to the Harvest
by Ben R. Peters

Available from Kingdom Sending Center
www.kingdomsendingcenter.org

Resurrection!
A Manual for Raising the Dead
by Ben R. Peters

Available from Kingdom Sending Center
www.kingdomsendingcenter.org

Signs and Wonders
To Seek or Not to Seek
by Ben R. Peters

Available from Kingdom Sending Center
www.kingdomsendingcenter.org

With Me
A Captivating Journey Into Intimacy
by Ben R. Peters

Available from Kingdom Sending Center
www.kingdomsendingcenter.org

Holy Passion: Desire on Fire
Igniting the Torch of Godly Passion
by Ben R. Peters

Available from Kingdom Sending Center
www.kingdomsendingcenter.org

Birthing the Book Within You
Inspiration and Practical Help
to Produce Your Own Book
by Ben R. Peters

Available from Kingdom Sending Center
www.kingdomsendingcenter.org